FIND YOURSELF

FIND YOURSELF

Pravin Sharma

KALPAZ

ISBN: 978-93-5128-025-5

Price: ₹ 290

First Published 2013

Published by

Kalpaz Publications
C-30, Satyawati Nagar,
Delhi - 110052
E-mail: kalpaz@hotmail.com Ph.: 9212142040

Laser Typesetting: Rajender Vashist, Delhi
Printed at: G. Print Process, Delhi

Cataloging in Publication Data--DK
Courtesy: D.K. Agencies (P) Ltd. <docinfo@dkagencies.com>

Sharma, Pravin.
Find yourself / Pravin Sharma.
p. cm.
ISBN 9789351280255

1. Self-actualization (Psychology) 2. Self culture. I. Title.

DDC 158.1 23

Contents

	Insight Thoughts	9
1.	Life	11
2.	Relation	15
3.	Problem	18
4.	Worship	24
5.	Religion	28
6.	Believe	32
7.	Work	35
8.	Organisation	40
9.	Home	44
10.	Love	47
11.	Friend	50
12.	Marriage	53
13.	Baby	56
14.	Test	62
15.	Interview	67
16.	Money	70
17.	Cheating	74

18. Corruption 78
19. Character 81
20. Profession 84
21. Innovation 87
22. Book 89
23. Law 91
24. Jealous 95
25. Inspiration 98
26. State of Mind 101
27. Interaction 104
28. Personality 106
29. Writing 110
30. Motivation 112
31. Patience 118
32. Comfort 120
33. Music 122
34. Time 124
35. Management 127
36. Precaution 130
37. Freedom 132
38. Prison 135
39. Change 139
40. Peace 141
41. Politics 143

42. Wise and Fool 148
43. Memory 152
44. Stress 154
45. Crowd 157
46. Target 159
47. Stairs 162
48. Opinion 164
49. Confession 166
50. Weapon 168
51. Fear 171
52. Idle 174
53. Differences 176
54. Addiction 178
55. Tears 180
56. Death 182

Insight Thoughts

- Clarity of ideas can be judged from your uninterrupted speech.
- To keep a healthy relationship with someone you have to be transparent.
- Limitation of thinking proves that you love your success least.
- If you want to live after your death, live in the heart of others, then you will never die.
- If you make a person realize his mistakes, you have made him bold, enough to face them.
- If you want to see change in your life, you have to change your thinking.
- If you define yourself with fools, they will redefine you.
- We are responsible for our mistakes because we never think before we commit, but we do think after we commit.
- Your ability to do reasoning shows that you don't want to take things for granted.
- It has a difference of miles to give pain to someone and to feel pain for someone.
- Your views are the roots of your development.
- Ifs and buts are the word, which discourages you from doing experiments in your life.

- A good suggestion at the right time can make you happy for the lifetime.
- Silent love is the feeling that you can feel till your death. To express your love you have to break this silence and its loud should hit the eardrums and increase the beat of your heart. If silence remains silent, it makes your heart violent. So, break this silence and say, I LOVE YOU.
- "I have to prove myself the best and for that I have to break my last record."
- I criticize myself to believe that I am incomplete.
- Wise people think from brain, fools think from heart but the evil doesn't waste their lives in thinking.
- If we knew that we are going to lose the game then its better to fight, to lose, by the least.
- Positive thoughts are the perceptions of positive attitude.
- Believing in yourself; lead you to attain success after many failures.
- When people don't want to listen you; listen to yourself and move ahead.
- When you attain the Height of success; you can play with the permutations and combinations of different failures.

Pravin Sharma

1

Life

Truth of life is what? What is truth? What is the meaning of truth? Then, what is lie? Why do we lie? How do we feel, when we lie? You know, again the only two words, which we had first learnt in our childhood recall at our last. But we use it with our interest, by calculating our profit and our gain first. Don't you think so? It's true.

We don't feel shy, when we lie. But we do feel pride when we speak truth, isn't so, when we have been taught at our childhood, the differences in the two. The difference remains there throughout our life. We know from our heart, the meaning of the two, the differences of the two, and the result of the two also, but still we don't hesitate to lie. We never think about the result, when we lie. We do this with 100-per cent risk. If it materializes, we feel happy, if its not, we search for another.

We start our life at this, we end our life at this but we never realize, our lie could kill a person, could destroy him but still we are happy. Getting favourable result by speaking a lie is the same as living a life by inhaling polluted air. In both the cases, you won't live longer. We do understand every pro and cons when we speak lies, our faces also don't support our soul, but still we do it.

Getting a favourable result for ourselves is the only motto, while we do it but why we do it, is not clear to us. We want a quick result from our efforts. We don't want to lose even a single chance. By hook or crook, we are interested with only favourable results.

With every endeavour we want maximum despite of our effort being incomplete. We don't want to lose, we don't want to retry and we don't want to waste our time in thinking for the right way, for our effort to get the good result. But we pay less time in thinking of the short cut for our result. Sometimes, we are in light and sometimes in the dark, in the cell.

The shortcut could lead you to a long darkness of your life. So why don't you prefer for a long and a planned way, systematic way, to have your life in brightness instead of darkness. You have only one life to live, but you have two options truth or lie.

The two have entirely different worlds; different descriptions and you are only one and having only one life to live, that too, having countable years to live. We don't know about our end, we just live our lives and feel happy, when we cheat others and feel sad when being cheated. Don't you think this is a bitter fact of life?

For whom are we cheating and for what are we cheating? Can't we live our life by speaking truth; by facing the world and saying "I cannot sell myself for pennies"? "My life is valuable for me and I won't sell my soul for any bad practice."

I know it's tough to live in this world, with good idealism but it is good to feel that you are an idealistic person. "*Short-term gains are never permanent and long-term takes a long time to prove so*".

Your zeal towards your endeavour should be firm that you will take your task, with your heart and your soul and never let yourself down for all those practices, which are not meant for a good soul.

You know for every question, there is only one answer and it ends there, if the answer is right or you have spoken the truth. But if it is a lie, it starts with never ending questionnaires. In the end, you, will feel puzzled with yourself, and with your answers, and the questions from where you had started. Life has been given to us, to love not to cheat others.

It's tough to speak truth but it is toughest to face the world and your soul with lies. You cannot define yourself, describe yourself, if you lie, on the other hand you don't have to define yourself, describe yourself, because the truth needs no definition, no description. Truth is itself the question and the answer. You will feel yourself happy, only happy at the last stage of your life that you were clear with the meaning of truth and lie. You will die happily and people will remain in love with you after your death.

2

Relation

We start our life at "A" and till we attain at "Z" we come across many relations in our life. Some of them are personal, some are official, and we have different definitions for the two. But very few of us do really understand the "R" of the relation. Why so? To keep a person in our life or to maintain the relationship, just for the sake of obligation has no meaning, not at all. We live in illusion and want to remain in illusion, we never try to come out of it, but by mistake, if some day something happens to us, we feel shattered for that person, whom we had loved most in our life, who told us the definition of life, definition of relationship. Why do we wait to know the answer from others, instead find it on our own. The person, who will answer you, may be more stupid than you, then why do you not prove yourself wise, in time, without losing anything and feel happy that you have saved yourself from getting cheated, from someone, whom you know.

Whomsoever we meet in our life, in our day-to-day work, we always try to develop a positive relationship with them, feel secured with them, never in our dream, we think negatively of them and that is now one start to trust, and have faith in a good human being. If we exercise our analytical brain and think about the symbol of negative, it is "-" and the symbol of positivity, it is "+", so if you want to make positive, you have to make negative first, don't you think so? Meaning that, if you make him negative first, you will be safe, because if at all he was negative, you already knew about it and if it was positive, there was nothing to harm you. This doesn't mean you develop negativity with you but since precaution is always better than cure, you have your right to put yourself in safe hands by analyzing the two identities.

Strategies are meant for us, principles and policies are made by us, for our own benefit. Only a few in this world want to help without seeking anything in return. We say that, he is a good person and for the same, worse, when we get cheated by the same, we feel disgusted, because it is very difficult to believe that, whom we knew to be good is bad, because when we feel ourselves cheated by the same person, we find ourselves no where.

We cannot apologize to ourselves, because it was our trust, our faith and our relation, with that person, and more or less, we are solely responsible for whatever happened with us. It is never too late now, to think again that, who am I? Who are you? And the reason for which we are together.

How much do I understand myself at that moment, of my life, what should I think of myself, for my trust and for my mistake, which I did by trusting you, only trusting you. Only feeling ashamed of myself that I trusted you. It's never too late, to think again the "R" of the relation and have the answers to all the questions. If you sought for a healthy relationship, this doesn't mean everybody would have healthy senses too. So, before getting involved with anyone in your life, think twice because you can be wrong.

3

Problem

It is very difficult to get out of every problem in our lives or otherwise we won't have any work left to do in our lives and that's the reason Almighty has given problem to every one, whom He trusts. We have to fight; to get rid of a problem no. 1, 2, and 3 and so on till the end of our lives and the meaning of life is more or less the same.

Having plenty of problems means Almighty want to draw your attention towards Him often, because all the time when you will fight, you will remember Him, pray to Him and seek help from Him. You know very few of us really understand the meaning of the problem but everybody seeks for a good and a favourable solution for oneself. Why so? Solutions are embedded in the problem itself but very few can distinguish it. We feel ourselves tired, in pain, when we are in problem our face values change and the reverse, when we find a solution. So, don't you think, life is like a pendulum and you have to go through it, by any means possible.

Fighting with the problems is the best and the most suitable solution. You don't have to borrow anything to fight for it; neither do you need someone to fight for you. It is always good, to analyse your problem with the best of your skills and put yourself solely responsible, for its solution also. As the problem is yours so, you should get the credit for your efforts in getting the solution.

When we find ourselves with a problem, it's human nature that we share our pain with someone or everyone. Without realizing this, that what does he make of you? How much positive is he, with you? How much concern, does he have for you, with your problem? But we waste our time, in explaining to everyone, whom we come across in our life, and very few come forward to guide us or listen to us, with an open heart. Otherwise a problem remains the problem and you are said to be the creator of the problem. If you seek for a good solution, for yourself then why don't you analyse the problem yourself? If you define the problem, then you are having the best solution for it too. If you understood the cause of the problem then nobody else in this world can give a better reply to it, than you.

We feel light, when we discuss our problem and feel heavy, when we have a problem but how do we feel, when we get the solution, lighter or lightest or none. I think it is none because on getting the solution, we just become happy and forget all that heaviness or lightness, which we had felt during the problem.

Finding the solution or having a good discussion to get a solution is the best effort to resolve the problem. A problem in itself has a very limited arena but we take it beyond boundaries, because of the evil that is inside us. Nothing is permanent in this life, so, how could a problem be so? Things are like this; people don't want to have a healthy discussion otherwise a healthy discussion is more or less a partial solution. If we are able to understand the problem, I think we are very near to its solution. Calling for a meeting for having a discussion is same as challenging the problem, but getting a result from the discussion solely depends upon, how much open you are to others opinions? You have to lose something, to get the solution. If you will not lose, how could he get or if he will not lose how you could get?

Basically, it is only the changing of platform, for a better present, future and to kill the evil past. With the problem, you won't live happily neither will you die happy. So, why don't you leave it for the two?

Sometimes fighting for your right becomes the only solution at that moment, if you do not fight, they will consider you as coward and cowards are never given their rights willingly. So, when fighting is the only solution of the problem then it is better to fight, till your death and to prove that nothing can be imposed on you forcibly.

If your soul is not allowing you, never compromise with anything. It is better to see the result of your action than to feel or think at the last stage of your life, that if you would have done this, what would have been the result, and at that moment you will only feel sorry for your late decision. Don't you think so?

Sometimes we do understand the problem but we never discuss with the person with which it is associated. We think that time will tell his mistakes to him and we keep on viewing, analysing the problems without discussing with the concerned person. We feel he could be hurt; he could take me wrong, my good relation with that person would get spoiled, because of this; we start hiding his mistakes, problems and inviting problems for ourselves.

Living with the problem and with the person and not even telling him, is same as stabbing your love on his back, because if you love him, you would be the first to tell him and if he loves you, then he will definitely put his brain to think, why you, the most important person in his life, has said so, is really something wrong with him. Persons who are close to others can see mistakes, problems clearly and have the solutions for it too. But it is always good to tell the mistakes and problems on the face and to make him realize that you don't want to see him in a difficult situation tomorrow, so be aware today.

Find it, get it and solve it, before it dissolves you, in itself. Fighting with one or two is easier than to fight with many. Never lose your brain or temperament while fighting otherwise it will be an addition of one more problem in your life. You are not the one who is fighting with it, but you are among many, who are doing so? If you do not fight, you will be crushed by it. Your identity could be in danger so to save yourself or if you love yourself, just do it and feel happy with the result.

Very few of us have this zeal to fight; otherwise many of us compromises with the problem just to avoid another. The two have different meaning, different direction and different results too. Now only you could better reply which one you want to opt?

Sometimes compromise is the best solution of any problem but it should be taken as healthy, otherwise it won't last long and you will fight again. People who are not clear from their heart will never have a healthy solution for their problem, so again we have to judge ourselves and to find, is there something wrong with me, am I totally right, am I responsible for it, or am I the problem itself? If you find yourself responsible for the problem just come forward and become the solution too, before it becomes too late and you find yourself no where.

4

Worship

We say that the worship is the media to attain God, to call Him when we need, when we require Him, in our lives, in our problems. But do you think we really know the meaning of worship, meaning of God, and meaning of the Almighty.

I think we are incomplete from our heart. We don't know the meaning of worship or the way of worship, to get our Almighty, not for the moment, when we seek Him the most, but for the entire hours during which we live.

You know everybody has different reasons to call God, his worship has a specific interest and it varies from person to person. He is interested with his interest, not with the interest of the person, who is also like him. He seeks to fulfill his desires, his needs and keeps on praying to God that 'Hey Almighty, please do listen to me, my call from my heart. I'm in need of you and give me the best in my life. I will keep on praying you, till the end of my life'. Is this the meaning of worship, to attain your God, and do you think, he will listen to you when you call? No not at all, Why so?

Calling with the interest has no meaning, calling with the interest of the masses has some meaning and calling with having no interest is full of meaning. He has the power to understand that why are you calling him and the reason behind it. It is true we call Him in our need and forget Him at our best. He feels alone at that moment of joy, when you were happy, you hadn't invited Him, and in pain you called Him first. Why this discrimination for Him, for our Almighty. Don't you think we are very mean in getting credit for us? It's true, we always want to prove our superiority and here we fail again and again.

We are here in this universe to do work for our living and we don't have to say that I am superior or should seek for credit. Just go on working, without any interest. You will find things are well tuned and people have started liking you.

No doubt, worship is the media, channel to pursue God, the only way to call Him, but where do I make my call? Where? Can you give me the answer of to this? God is said to be Almighty. He is omnipresent, in every soul but still we couldn't find Him. We do not have the eyes to recognize Him; we do not have enough sensitivity to feel Him.

You know we are willing to pay heavy amount to go to a distant shrine but we are unwilling to pay to a person, in genuine need. You know we feel happy, more than happy on our every visit to a distant shrine but we are least interested with the pain of the person, who is very close to our eyes? Why so? We don't count how much we spend on our journey, but we do count our interest in helping others.

Feeling for a person in problem, finding him in pain and thinking of him as a good person who might be crushed by some evil and taking him out of it, is the meaning of worship.

Even if you can't do anything for him but still if you have thought for him, felt for him, that he is in a problem, he is in pain, you have done your worship. Because Almighty would send someone else likes you, for him, to get him out of the problem.

He will not leave him in the problem but He has given you a chance to prove your love for Him.

We are very calculative in helping others, we are fast as computer to calculate our profit, we don't want to do anything for free and here we fail again. I am not saying not to charge your service, as every minute has a different definition of an hour. It starts for a second, then a minute, then an hour, then a day, night, week, month and a year. During this we come across many living beings and if we really know the meaning of worship, we should at least think once for that person, in pain and pray to the Almighty to save him or to take him out of the problem. Sometimes, we do understand the problem, pains of others, just try to remove it before he expects or tells you. Reading a face, reading a heart or reading a soul of a person in his pain and even thinking of him is the best way to make yourself special in front of you're the Almighty. He was there in that person and He had given you the power to help Him and to love Him. He is there with you and me, and evil is also there among very near to us. If you are clear in the definition of worship, you won't have to search for the God; He is there in you, while helping others, while crying for others, while feeling pain for others. If you find yourself, you will find Him too.

5

Religion

Religion the parameter within which we find ourselves confined in our thoughts and belief. Religion is the media to define your God and belief. All the religions have the same goal, same values of belief but we make something different, of its meaning, for our interest and kills the ethics of the sentiments of many.

What makes you to extrapolate the meaning of religion for your benefit? It's true we are attached to our religion with sentiments because of the belief that worship requires a platform to pray, to God. You can know the value of your prayer, if you have belief in all.

Confinement makes you narrow in your thinking and belief. So, make yourself clear from your soul that Almighty has no difference for you and him. It is only you, who has so? You have imposed your interest on him for your benefit and calculations. Otherwise all the religions have only one message for their disciples that love the mankind, humanity, you will find the Almighty in your heart.

We the intellectual class has divided the religion in many, but we forget the principle of religion. If you find yourself happy in the shadow of love, that is the most beautiful religion to adopt. Your evilness will move you towards your untimely death and make you the reason of your death. A healthy thought will make you live with senses so, believe in the belief that makes you to believe in yourself, that you are clear in your perception of religion.

Caste makes a sense, if it is being done for the humanity otherwise; it is nonsense to fight for it. Racial discrimination between white and black, differentiation between poor and wealthy shows only our immaturity of mind that we are still confined in our incomplete thoughts.

A good soul full of love and care is a person to be loved, irrespective of his caste, religion and color. He is complete, as a human and you have lots of things to learn from him and for that you have to believe that, the person and his personality is the best asset for him, to prove his existence.

If I cannot understand the pain of the person, I am not a religious person. Religion makes no differences, if the person is in problem. Today he is in need; tomorrow you could be so, put yourself in his position and understand the value of religion.

You are more important than your religion and if you believe that we make religions in our interest and the value of a person is important to feel; we will not compare the two. A person from a different religion, different caste but having thoughts on development, for the mankind, is not confined to one religion, but his thoughts make him different and valuable for all. Don't make yourself egoist in defining the meaning of religion, for your interest and benefit.

Making use of the meaning for the sake of the personal interest and to involve the masses, to divert them from the theme of the religion, shows that you can kill anybody, for your interest. No religion teaches us to fight, but still we fight, this shows, you have made it personal and without thinking of the values it teaches you.

You cannot find yourself in peace, if you don't know the meaning of pain, love and care. Religion elevates your mind to give a direction of your belief for the purpose of making your soul bright. You will find yourself spiritual, if you believe in the religious thoughts, your happiness has a relation with your mind, your mind has a relation with your soul and your soul has again relation with your religion. Never kill the ethics of the religion because your soul has a relation with it and you won't find yourself happy, if your thoughts have evilness.

I pray to God to make myself good to feel the pain, to sense the tears and giving me the power, to take care of them in their need. Define the religion for the betterment of the mankind, to uplift the soul of the person to make him feel that his personal interest won't have much importance, when there is the matter of the mass. If your religion makes you confined in your thoughts then you might have understood regional and not religion widen your senses to understand the meaning of it.

6

Believe

Believe and belief is not only the words but it is a start of the faith on the mankind, humanity. It's our weakness that we believe and we feel responsible for our weakness, when somebody hurts our trust. But this is also a fact that we have to believe, on at least someone otherwise it's very difficult to live.

Always feel insecure in the company of others, other than yourself and whom you can trust. Never believe in blind faith, if the Almighty has given you clear vision to judge the best for you. Don't call problem in the shape of faith with a stranger, whom you met just on the way. All people are not bad; simultaneously all of them are not even good. So, whom do you trust? If you believe in yourself, you won't have to believe in anyone else and then you would have fewer problems than others.

We believe in God, we are in search of him, till our end, we pray at the temple, we pray in mosque, we never think bad in the premises of temple, mosque but just coming out of the premises in a fraction of seconds, we find ourselves in the same malpractices. We have been told that he is omnipresent but we don't feel afraid of him, while committing the sin. Why so? This shows we are not clear on our belief in him. Isn't so? Until you find yourself similarly in the temple, as in general places, you will find yourself incomplete in your belief. Temple or mosque can be made in any place in the world but if you will differentiate them, you won't find him. Make yourself clear in your belief, you will find all the holy places are there with you and you were puzzled with something else. You know the best way of doing worship is to love mankind, humanity and feel pain for them, who are also like you, a creature made by the Almighty.

People, the saints, who speak on the definition of God, worship and call masses to hear them, are only the messengers of God, they have understood to some extent, the meaning of God and its existence. They are the better orator and know your weakness, regarding the subject and they describe it, so beautifully that we take them as our God.

We started doing worship of a person who has the same biological features as we have. Life has to end one day and that we don't know, when and how? So if nobody is clear about his end. Then we should believe in someone, whom we never met but find him in our soul, when we take care of someone in his need, feel pain from our heart, and find a solution for his problem. Your, faith and belief in the Almighty is complete.

7

Work

Why do we work? What for? Is it for the bread and butter, to make our life healthy, to live our lives with a command? But how do we feel, with our work, happy or just happy. If it is just happy, then it means, we are working, otherwise, if we do really love our work, we don't have to work for even a day. It will become a stream of life, with this zeal that every moment, in which we are living, we are living in total. If you are not happy with your work, profession, it's the same as killing yourself.

Loving your work is the same as loving your life. Do understand your work, before you start your work, then you don't have to work till the end of your life. Getting older is not in your hand but making a good shape of your life is in your hand. You don't have to regret at the end of your life that you wasted it, this precious life, given by Almighty to you. Many of us have realised this problem in their life that they are not doing work in which they are happy. But still they compromise with their profession their life and feel puzzled, depressed through out of their lives and slowly kill themselves till their last breath.

Living a healthy life is your right, for living you have to work, it's mandatory. So why don't you think, to live happy and to adopt the work in which you find yourselves comfortable. Then you will not be in tension; depression and you will find you are living every moment of your life.

Living healthy not only depends upon good food but have a contribution of good and positive thoughts, good environment, healthy discussions and a good job or work. Then you will find yourself happy at your workplace and at home, people among you will always consider you as a helping hand. You won't bring your office problems at your home and feel good that you are the lucky one, who don't have a headache from the day's work. "Work is Worship". Do you know the meaning of it? yes if, God is there in you otherwise you were searching for Him in vain.

Doing worship is the work to attain God. But if we do respect our work, we are again worshiping the same Almighty because when we do it, we definitely come across, many people in our life. If we were healthy in our senses while working, people will love us, they will give regard to us and care for us, at that time the Almighty was there with you with your positive attitude, caring for others. Is not true?

You don't have the right to kill yourself so think again do you really love your work, understand your work. If yes, there is life ahead of you, to develop yourself otherwise you don't have time. So, hurry up what are you waiting for? He has given you a brain, use it for your sake and start a new life. You will always find yourself to be the loving one, good one, creative one, healthy one and for everyone.

With every endeavour of your life, you will find that your zeal to cope up with your problem have become an example for others. If you are not clear with the meaning, the definition of work, you are engaged with. Better to stop it, then and there, otherwise it will become too late for you, to know the meaning of life. When you work, people take you positive or negative. You should be less interested with their negativeness, if your senses are positive. You should stick to your positiveness and to go ahead with your effort. Their ness negativeness will kill them and your positiveness will develop you. So, where are you lost ? You have your birthright, to think about yourself and you are not doing anything wrong if you care about yourself.

People with the same kind of thinking always turn to be good friends and the different minds are foes. It's true, you are happy with them, who have same likings, same thoughts, and it is always good to associate with them for your development, your creativity and your peace of mind. No need to proceed with whom you are not clear, with work, with the relation, with anything which has any link with your life. Leave now, for your better tomorrow, understand now what's wrong with it. Can't you live without it? If yes, then you have the answers to all the questions. You yourself are intelligent enough, to give the answers of every question but you seek answers from others and in this, your life comes to an end. Start loving yourself, you will find, everything well tuned, smooth and you can understand the philosophy of life.

Living a life has no meaning, if you are not clear that why are you living? Why are you working? Are you happy with your work, with your profession? Do you love to be loved by all? Do you regret for your mistakes that can hurt someone? Do you know the relation of life and work? Why work is worship? How can we make ourselves prosperous and kill too? We are solely responsible for everything because we have our own identity and if we love it, care for it. We will definitely see to it, then when we are wrong and on finding anything odd, we will have to rectify it, too. We won't be given a second chance by Almighty to change ourselves, because if we can't love ourselves then we can't love anyone else in this world. If you love yourself, it means at least you know the meaning of love and you can well define it to others too. So, start loving yourself first and feel happy with your good start. If you will love yourself, you will not ditch yourself. If you don't want to ditch yourself, then you will definitely put your life forward in the right direction for a better pursuit of life.

Living a life with all the definitions clear in the mind, in the heart, in the soul, is like traveling on the road heading towards your home. You don't have to ask, the address of your own home. So, make your life clear in all perceptions so that it gives a meaning for every minute in which you are living and you want to live.

It makes a sense to think before death because after it there is nothing to think upon. Be clear, you only have one life; you could be the creator or destroyer of it. So, never compromise on getting a clear meaning of life. You have to answer yourself at the end of your life? Don't you think so?

8

Organisation

We start our day at our office with a task, for a result and with the end of the day, in the evening, we feel free, its time to go to home and we start our next day again in the same mode. But do we really utilize every minute of our day, in our office for the work. I think not. We do our work, because we are bound to do so, otherwise we won't have pending files on our table. We don't feel sorry, for what we did not accomplish today, but we do feel happy, if we don't have work.

We feel scared, if the boss is in the cabin and feel relaxed, if he is out. Why a boss is the boss? A person having the same biological feature as you have is different from you, in his thinking, in his style, in his method of problem solving and his dedication towards work, which you don't have, is the quality of the boss.

If you are clear with your task, know your responsibilities and the relation between

Employees—Work—the Employer. You don't feel scared of anything, neither of the boss nor of the work. You will love to do work, because this the only tool by which you can carve yourself, for your better present and your tomorrow. Very few understand this relationship.

Take this as you are working for yourself, to make yourself for your better tomorrow, you have completed your task before time and engaged with another one. A person with these qualities cannot be put behind the curtain and your work will make a special space for you for your dedication.

We never feel satisfied about what we are getting from the company and so we work halfheartedly and the result we never get more than what we are getting.

You have to make it clear to your company about you, your interest, and your work and give them their time to think about you, because you are not an ordinary person. If a company is getting profit because of you, then you have your full right to ask for your share. Every employer should have this thing clear in his mind that each and every employee associated with him is valuable and the Almighty has given him this power to love them, give them bread for their food, so they are also not an ordinary person.

It's teamwork; no company can run without good

employees. Profit cannot be earned without dedication to your work. You cannot get love without loving others. Very few get this chance to become the employer and to be loved by his employees. You will feel like working in heaven, if your employer cares for you and you treat his company as your mother. If working is the only tool to carve our life then why don't we prefer to work with our full potential?

We will find ourselves healthy, supportive and enthusiastic, if we are punctual with time and committed to work.

There are two types of activities in which we engage ourselves. They are TWA, i.e., Time Wasting Activities and VPA, i.e., Value Producing Activities. We have brains in our head but we almost forget this, when we kill our time. All of us do work but very few of us, do really understand that how to work? Don't you find its difference, why only few not everyone! The reason, people don't want to complete their task, their approach and because of short-term gains they spoil their long-term achievements. Only few have the patience to wait for their better tomorrow. If you have thought to live for tomorrow also do plan everything, your relation, your work, your love, your enemy, everything. You will find you are living in a system and you are living a planned life.

Whenever you make plans, you should plan everything; all ifs and buts have to be removed before you start but when you work, you should work without ifs and buts, otherwise you won't be able to work. Working with the hope of a good result can disappoint you on the result. So, it's better to work with full effort and to think that nothing was left in your effort. The Result will definitely be yours. *"If we knew that we are going to lose the game then its better to fight, to lose by the least"*.

It seems the organisation is only a word but it has a meaning for those, who knew that this is the place where we spend our maximum time of our lives, when we are at the stage and the age of the healthy potential brain. So, why don't we make ourselves complete with the meaning of an employer, employee and the organisation?

9

Home

Home is the best place for me in the world. There is peace, there is love, and there is everything for me to make me feel that there is something missing, when I am away from my home. It is not only the walls which make a home but care and love of the persons and their healthy relations make a home, a sweet home.

Giving importance to the view or the liking, to listen in the interest of the family members is giving regard and respect to the elder or the younger, to make him feel that, he is important for all.

You can not live happy happily in your home, if any of the members is not satisfied with your decision, if you have not taken him in confidence, by asking him, his decision, his interest. You cannot make your home happy, if you feel that the persons living in it as less important. Even a baby has his right giving suggestions as an elder, to make him feel that he is important; his views have an importance to come to any conclusion.

Decisions related to your home is to be taken with the support of all the members living in it, to make them feel the part of the decision, otherwise you are said to be a dictator, imposing your good or bad decisions on them. You love to sleep on your bed with your pillow because you find yourself comfortable with it rather in an expensive suite of a hotel. Your mind feels peace; your body feels relaxation from the exertion and your soul feels love to find your loved ones. Make them happy to make your home a heaven because you have to live in it, for the whole of your life.

It is the dream of everybody to have a home for him, in his life. You should plan it, by every means so that, you get the best place in the world. Your wall of the house should be built by the bond of love. Roof of the house should be there to take care of the people living under it. Doors should have the symbol of respect and the windows should have the thoughts, which widen horizons.

A complete home makes an essence with the persons living in it and its meaning is having a relation relationship with them. If you are not happy with your relations then your home would not be a sweet home, you won't find yourself in the home, being in the home, your presence makes no sense because there is something, someone has entered in your home, without your will and has disturbed the environment. You are solely responsible for living in hell, if you have never tried to make it heaven. You have to put your effort, to make your dream home, a place, where there is a shadow of love, a vision of brightness in the thoughts and shelter of care.

There could not be any place in the world where you find yourself relaxed other than your home, so make the place, the better, to live your life healthy. There should not be any noise, even from the doors that can make your sleep disturbed. Your hell and heaven can be your home, if you have not made yourself clear with the meaning of home and the persons living in it.

10

Love

Love is the most beautiful and sweet word of this world. Life has a meaning, if you know the meaning of love. You won't be alone; neither will you be sad, if you are sure about the depth of love. It's hard to measure the depth from the top, to know, you have to fall in it and the beauty of this word is that you will never want to come out of it.

To love a person in your life is the necessity of your life, to get love of a person is the requirement of your life. On finding someone, as your love, you will find, you were incomplete before and now you know the meaning of life.

To have a healthy relation with someone, you have to be transparent. If you hide your identity, personality and nature, you won't develop a healthy relation. Love is a matter of chemistry and you will feel the reactions to the actions of your care, caress and hug.

You won't find the person in problem, if he knows

the meaning of love, because it makes him sensitive and caring to understand the state of mind. Those who are unaware of its sweet touch or does not understand the meaning of love; they just fight for nothing, to end their identity.

You could live in the heart of others, if you know its meaning. This small word has a depth of an ocean, vast as the sky and the meaning of life. You will find a good discussion; with a good spirit having fragrances of love has resolved your disputes with your enemy. it takes years for you to stand on your feet, but it takes a second to kill someone, after that he will never wake up or stand up.

You too, also running for your life might get yourself killed by anyone, anytime. So, why don't you believe in this principle that you will love to resolve your disputes than to be killed by them?

If you believe in a good heart, a stable and wise mind, you will never compromise with the ethics of life. Make them feel that, it is not only your problem but you are here to resolve it, with them. If they are not clear then define so that they can understand what the basic problem is and what is the status of the problem? Does this problem really have any sense? If not, then what you are fighting for ?

Let's be in love and feel the difference, you will realize that, you have lost a precious time in fighting and that won't come again. Believe in the theory of love, that, more you spread its fragrance, more you beautify your life. Then you will find that your life has a meaning to live and you will love to be loved by all. Do come forward in finding yourself and making yourself clear that, you won't let your life go, just like that. You want to make it specific for yourself and for all. "If I love myself then I won't kill the meaning of love. I will define for you, till my end."

11

Friend

Friend is a nice word, a nice personality, whom we meet in our life, for sharing, caring and to love till the end of our life. We feel more pain for someone, whom we consider our friend friends , in his problem than to a person, with whom; we have the relation of blood. Is it not true?

We want to spend maximum time in the company of them, because we feel our self-happy with them. It's a human tendency that, we never go to that place, where we find ourselves in complex relations, but we cannot stop the time, with a person, with whom, we want to spend, some more time.

We feel sorry, when we depart from him and feel pain, for him, in our day-to-day life. This is what the definition of a friend. Then why don't we make our relation, as friends, with our father, mother, brother, sister, your loving wife and your children too. You will definitely find that you love to be at home than to be in a party with a stranger.

Make yourself clear, explain yourself in totality with them, give regard, respect to them, do feel their pain in the problem, discuss their needs, interest, feel free to speak, your negatives, demerits, give them reward, hug, caress on their achievements and discuss everything with them, to make them feel, that you are incomplete without them. You will find you have healthy friends to take care of your pain.

"A friend in need is a friend indeed", we all know this but we do not prove it all. We make ourselves transparent to him, in our relation but he, whom we love most in our life, sometimes proves something else. Finding a friend having love and care is difficult to find. But on finding him, never lose him, it's rare. It's our weakness that the males are attracted to females and females to males. We feel delighted in the company of opposite sex. We feel happy to talk to them, to share our problems, to discuss ourselves with them. This is because of the attraction from the opposite sex; its natural and you don't have any right to prove it wrong. Find a friend, from the opposite sex, you will find, he or she absorbs half of your problem and you will feel relaxed to discuss with him or her. As long as you maintain the dignity of friendship and feel the pain of your friend, you will find you will never be alone.

Very few are lucky, who can say, they have true friends, but many say we are friends. No need to involve yourself with a person, whom you assume as a friend but his traits are of a stranger. Tomorrow he could teach you a lesson on friendship so, be aware of the meaning of friends and put yourself in safe hands.

12

Marriage

Marriage is the relation between the two, starting of a new life, with full of joy and caring for each other. But why do we marry? Do we really understand the meaning of it? We just want to marry, but for what? Can you give me the answer to this? If not, then there is something for you and for your beloved. People are not clear with the meaning, but they do it, simply do it, to get the pleasure of copulation, for the lifetime. Is it what the meaning of marriage? No not at all. Then, what is the meaning of marriage?

We share everything but still sometimes we are unable to clear ourselves, till our end. We have our day, our night and the whole of our life, but still, we find ourselves incomplete. Why so? This is also a truth that sometimes we were not clear with the meaning, but has a baby in our hand. What was the mistake of that baby, who is being brought by you, when you were not clear with the relation, with your love?

You have to make yourself clear with your love, by every means. You have to tell that you are my weakness. You have to discuss from A to Z of your life, as a friend of a lifetime. Taking into confidence, loving to remove each other's problems, to make each other happy, and to feel like that you can't live without each other; you are the need of each other's life. You will find you are living with a person, who is your friend, your life partner. You will find, your home has now become heaven and you know the meaning of love now.

If your life partner is not educated, illiterate, then you have to do extra exercises, to tell, to guide, to educate, to make life better. Discuss yourself, your work, your day and your night. You will feel happy that you have your partner for the lifetime to share your sorrow; your pain and you both are planning to make your life better. If you will discuss, you will find love in it. No doubt with your effort you will face changes in your life.

You should make it clear that your home cannot be your office; you have to put them apart to live happy. Try to resolve your differences with your love, make yourself clear in all the definitions of married life and search for happiness with your full support, you will find, you both were fighting, to be happy and to live with each other. Fighting with someone, whom you love most in your life, again shows, how much you love, care, your love to live for a lifetime, for caring, for loving and sharing for every sorrow and happiness together.

13

Baby

Baby the sweet gift of your married life, to live your life again, from your childhood. You can see your childhood, in his eyes and in his development with the time. You have been given another opportunity to make yourself complete without your mistakes, what you have done in your life, not to be repeated again, in the life of your child.

He is dependent on you, for your experience, good and bad both; you won't ditch him, as others can. He believes in you, you have to take care of him as a friend, teacher and a good father. Take him in confidence with you, so that he describes himself, with you and does not hesitate, to tell you the fact, the problem.

A person never hides from himself. So, make him feel that you and he are the same and both of you, will fight, to get rid of the problem. Make him feel that you are his best friend, as a father and make him realize that, you can not see him, in problem and will save him from his mistakes.

An association of a relation between you and him would lead you to feel that both of you cannot live without each other. A friend in your house, with the zeal of friendship and care, will make you feel the fragrance of love. You will have a confident relation with him and courage to fight for him.

He too, will feel good in your company and you feel lucky to hear his problems first. He will not hide anything from you, but describe the fact and his effort, with you. Knowing of his problem and his interest, makes you capable, to give him the right suggestion and approach to make him confident with his efforts. Then, he will love to share everything with you and feel confident that you are there, to take care of his interest and his problems.

Expectations are your desires from your child but don't compel him. He will give you, his best. Your expectation could be higher than your child's leap, he is too young to understand the meaning of killer instinct, make him realize that, and his participation gives you equal happiness, as fighting for the first.

You can make him understand that runner-ups have this option to beat, their records, in their next attempt. So, don't feel killed, with the failure and never lose your confidence.

A supportive attitude will make you develop his personality and he will never compromise, with the participation. Give him the confidence to express himself with you and never forget to give him the sweet touch, bye kiss, and hug.

Developing confidence in him, is putting him on the right track, to fight with his endeavours. Failure is the part of the life, if you won't fail, you would not find anything different in the taste of success, with your best opinion regarding the definition of success and failure, he will love to be your son and student.

If you will pay interest, to listen to him from your busy schedule, he will find love and care in it, a trust develops with your relation and he will not find himself alone in the home, when you are away from your work. But he will wait for your return, to tell you the entire episode and your interest will develop boost in him, to narrate the story with full enthusiasm.

He will find a friend in you and you will find love in him, you both have your interest, to make each other happy. So, develop a healthy relationship to make the meaning of relation complete. If you pay with your time today, he will not depart from you tomorrow, with your opinions, approach and interest. You will find him, till your end, for you, with you and you have the meaning of tears, pain, and clear in your heart and soul.

Live in the heart of him, he will never feel your death. Think of his mind and its creativity, to make him feel that his approach, have a sense but he has yet to learn many things from you. Don't impose your goodness on him, if he is not interested, he won't take it, adhere it, you also know this, until he feels himself that, you are not his enemy to kill him, but you are there, for him as an all time friend.

Until he feels himself wrong in his approach, habits, you won't able to change him, make him good. He will take you, as his enemy, your lecture on the topic will be wastage. So, make him feel that, he will be responsible for his death by his habits and you will cry that you could not save him.

You cannot change the person, until he feels guilty on his attitude. So, make him feel from his brain, because the development of his mind is also necessary to feel the difference between good and bad. Until you differentiate between the two, you won't be able to opt for good one. Make him answerable for his result and do ask him, his interest of work, so, that he never finds himself in a mould, set by you, for him. To Guide him, define him but make him solely responsible for his decision. So, that he never compromise with the zeal of his interest to perform. He will love your decision to make him feel confident with your guidance and feel happy to discuss with you, to analyse the best possible outcome from his effort. On his every success, he will give credit to you, for making a strong foundation for his life and getting him clear with the power of decision. He will be happy to have you, as his father and friend, and your clarity with the relation, will prove a good association.

Living a meaningful life with someone is having love forever. We have our different liking for a baby boy than a baby girl. We feel happy about having a boy than a girl. You might have found that in pursuit of having a boy, the family has seven children. The parents are not clear with their responsibilities, duties but they want to carry forward, their name with their son.

Development of discrimination becomes the part, in their feeling and giving them the best of your care and love, dissolves in your interest. Both of the creatures are having blood of yours, feeling of yours but still, you are liking to the boy than the girl. She also feels the differentiation, but to whom will she complain. She finds herself suppressed with her desires and incomplete in her identity because of your lack of interest in her development. You prove yourself businessman, while investing on the interest of your boy because you know, he will remain with you but the girl has to go, so taking care of her interest, would not be a gain. This shows our meanness that how much we love our blood and ourselves. You have been gifted a soul to love her and make her feel that she too can fight with the world, with her knowledge, guidance of yours and give fame to your name with her achievements. Then you will feel proud of yourself, being the father of a girl. Feel like a complete father, with the two and live your life with them to make them complete in their life.

14

Test

The Test is part of everybody's life. From our childhood to our end, we develop ourselves by learning and testing. It is the necessity to check you and to be checked by someone who taught you the basics.

Test is the stage before which you can consider yourself incomplete and after that, there is another goal to attain. It's a never-ending process before your death. You have to go through an examination everyday, if you want to develop yourself. Then why do we feel afraid of it, if it is mandatory to face, for a better result? The more you face examination, the more you become habituated to it and you will never be afraid of it.

From our childhood when we first had different books, different teachers of subjects we never liked all of them. Only a few are of our liking. Why we do not like all, only a few? We are good in some subject also we are bad in some, why we have the same liking for all? You know the reason behind it. Its fact, we like to hear a good story, as our subject. If the story is good we understand it, same for the subject. We all have the same capacity of the brain but we do require different exercises to maintain it. To Our liking or disliking of the subject depends solely on the first teacher, who had taught us, with his interest, concept and clarity, with the subject and the presence in the class.

Every subject which we start at our childhood and till we attain our youth has a link, has a relation and if by a mistake made by the teacher or by you, any link gets misplaced we find ourselves handicapped with the subject. Never take anything as understood from your teacher, at the time of his teaching, do ask everything to make attain clarity, with the synchronized story of your subject, otherwise you will have to pay with your career.

No subject could be tough as long as it is being taught like a story, like the flow of a river or stream. As river never flows in breaks, it flows in continuity; so, you have to adhere to it, for your development. When you opt a profession of teaching is a respect to the mankind because then you have been given power, to create a complete person. You should feel satisfied that you have got the opportunity to serve the mankind and you have to put your best effort for it. Half-heartedly working in this profession is a job of a killer, because then the student won't get the complete concept from you and their future will be spoiled, because of you.

You have no right to ruin the career of anyone, build them better and then feel good about yourself that you are in the foundation of this nation, this world and nobody could compared with you. It's hard to believe, but this is a fact. Tell your student, the meaning of the subject very clearly, without taking anything as understood to them. Feel like a student, think like a student and concentrate or put more stress at the point, where you think, there is much to discuss. You will find your class is full of students and they love to attend it. Discussion on the subject is the best tool to learn by heart and remember it, so, never forgets to call for an open dialogue discussion. You will always find the maximum result from it.

The best way to prepare any subject is to read, Remember, Recall and Retrieve, you will definitely have a good Result. All the R's might have the relation that is why the word has a meaning. Students who are not clear with the subject or the teacher, feel afraid of the subject, it is the duty of the teacher to take them in confidence and clear all their problems, through their own approach, understanding and to make them feel good with the result. They will start loving the subject and you. Your one good effort will make their lives forever and now they will love to face examinations.

Developing confidence in the student should be the prime motto of a teacher. Your presence is sought in the heart of your student and to make it, you have to prove it with your labour and dedication that you love your students, your profession and you want to make them complete so that every student gets the sprit to face examinations. Then they will never fail in their subject and you will never fail in your profession.

All the time when they will succeed, credit automatically comes to you, as you were in the foundation of their pillar. Some of them spoil the dignity of this profession; they just come to the school, college for Presence and Payment. They are least interested with their class; they start the topic from 'C' and end at 'T' with this assumption that the course is complete and they have done their job. Is this the meaning of teaching? Some of them are interested in the home tuition rather than to teach in the class.

Everybody can't afford to pay an extra tuition fee so, what was his or her fault, by being a student of yours. What the hell are you going to make with that few pennies? Building a career is the fulfilling of a dream, of a student, his parents, his family, you have been given a chance by the Almighty to do worship through this, if you will not avail, then you are the loser.

Do punish your student like anything, if you find them on the wrong track. Your punishment today will make their future tomorrow. They will realize this one-day and will repeat the same as you did with them. If you will tell them their tomorrow, today, with their likings, they will love to fight, to make it true. For this again, every word has to be understood about the subject with a relation, link, in a synchronized manner that, it is not for today, for which we are learning, it will be for the better tomorrow, so make it clear now to avoid any confusion.

Tomorrow, this could be possible, we won't have a teacher like you, and so it is better to learn everything from you, to make ourselves perfect. Always try to relate your theoretical knowledge with the practical aspects. Make yourself complete at the time of theory because either today or tomorrow, you are going to face it with practical problems. Practical knowledge does come from theory only, but we can get a good idea, if we relate the two, at the time of learning. Our interest in the subject also increases, because then we are able to know what practical problems we could face, when we enter a professional life. Knowing the answer, gives us the confidence at the very start of our career and you will find yourself competent enough to handle any problem.

15

Interview

We all know this; to face an interview is not an easy job. To get through it successfully is a difficult task and everybody has to face it and make efforts to clear it. This is a stage at which you are a stranger to the board and you have to prove them as knowledgeable, in a few minutes only.

You won't get an hour to define yourself or your skills, so with in a limited time, with your maximum positive effort, you have to prove them that you are the best. Face, voice, your diction, your dress sense, your trait, your regard, your presence of mind, a good IQ and your body language should be the part of your resume to make it complete for the presentation to the board. Sometimes your first step in the boardroom or sometimes your last word could make you get the job. Confidence in your face, in your voice gives a strong impact on the board and sometimes you are able to develop illusion in the board.

Always tell them, what they have asked; if you are clear instead to disgrace from the subject. If you do not understand the question clarify, your confusion instead of giving a confused answer. It's better to say sorry than to kill valuable time of the board. Do prepare yourself with whatever is written on your resume because you will be asked questions from there only.

Feel like you are in a disciplined room with your elders, where there is freeness to speak with the clarity of ideas, concept and a good experience. Nobody is perfect in this world, complete in this world, so if you don't know the answer of any question, it is not your fault. You might have not thought about it and as someone has asked you, now you will definitely search for the answer. With the experience we feel ourselves confident in our job. But try to get the right experience for the job.

Person busy for a number of years cannot be termed experienced, if he talks like a novice on the subject. If you are clear with the right approach, right concept, you are said to be an experienced novice and in a very short time, you will prove your caliber, quality. Fools don't have to describe themselves; they prove it, with their deeds. So, don't be afraid of, if you are not an experienced person, but do feel afraid of your bad experience, by killing your number of years, in your profession and still, you are a novice.

You don't have to be afraid of interview, take it as a meeting, for a discussion, about yourself and your work; make them clear with the best of your effort in the least time. You will definitely crack it. Be a good listener and feel comfortable with them in the board, you will definitely come out with a positive impact on the board.

16

Money

I want more; this desire comes to our mind, when we hear this word. This is not only a word for many of us, but a complete sentence of their life or the meaning of life is this and only this. We can go to any extent to get more money for us, irrespective the way we adopt. It makes us mad, it makes us sad and happy too, with the different phases of our life and we keep on running behind this, for this, till the end of our life.

We travel a lot we go to any part of the world, we kill our health and we kill others too, for only this. From the start of the life till the end of the life, we come across only this. So, you can say all the definition starts from you and ends at the money because relation, friendship, love, your work, desires, everywhere money is involved. You are good for your relation if you are wealthy, you are a good friend of mine, because you are rich, you are my first and last love because you spend much on me, you adopt malpractices to amass a good amount for you, your desire to get more, more than more, never comes to an end to this and in this, you end your life without living it healthy.

This is true, it is the need of the life but this is also true that it is not the only need of the life. You can make yourself with the money but this is also true that money can destroy you too. It makes you fight for your food, it makes you fight for your need, but it makes you fight for wealth too. It makes you blind, sometimes with your bad and wrong decision and makes you kill yourself. Money itself is everything, but nothing; it's an illusion that we think so; otherwise all the rich would have been the happiest persons on this earth. But we know this from our heart that, they are not so. They too have the problems as the poor man has, the difference is that they don't have money problems.

You can take as assets with you, to buy your needs, to fulfill your requirement, as a fighting tool from your problems and as a power, it is the need to fulfill your dream plans, to make your life run and to believe that the importance of money in life, is not important than life. You will get another chance to fulfill your dream but malpractice will sooner or later, lead you to behind the bars, there you won't find proper light, ventilation and your money, for which you did so.

Do fight for your right because if you were not clear then people will write to you, that you are an understood person. Then, you won't get anything in your life; neither money nor status and you are solely responsible for it. Money has a power to attract only those who are greedy, wise people do not run behind it; they make the way so that money flows to them. If you will make a good and healthy environment in your workplace, you will find, money inflow has increased but if you will work under pressure or not happy with your job, you won't have money.

Everybody wants to become wealthy, wants to attain power with this, a son is ready to kill his father, a wife is ready to ditch her poor husband, a person is ready to kill anyone for this, an old man at his last, still doesn't want to leave all this for the peace of his death. We are least interested with death but we are much happy to live for some time with money. It has always been seen that the money never makes a permanent place for it, it keeps on moving, like anything.

Today we are rich, tomorrow we could be poor and we don't know the cycle of it. So, we should make ourselves clear that if our attitude is positive, our altitude would definitely be high and then we won't have to run behind it, we will find something different in our case. Having much money, we have again become mad. It is really shameful for us that single word money and its meaning has a command on our life. Do use your brain; to come out of this illusion, you will never have the scarcity of money.

17

Cheating

Cheating is the dirtiest word in our life, but we are still adhering to it, for our profit, interest. Don't you think so? We can go to any extent for the sake of our profit. It's true, it's our need to get profit to maintain ourselves, but getting profit by cheating is not ethical.

We don't hesitate in cheating others but we do feel shattered on being cheated by someone else. Why so? We are ready to sell ourselves for anything. We are ready to kill anyone for anything. Why? Can you tell me, why? You cannot. From our childhood till our death, we are type cast. Everybody is ready to cheat others and in this cycle of life, we are the part of it. Don't you think so?

Getting more for us or everything for us, we do so? But for what, we are not clear. It's true, desires make us hungry but to get the food by wrong means is the same eating others' half eaten food. Knowingly, we never eat others' food then why for the interest, which might be the interest of someone else.

In our childhood, we cheat in our exams; we put more of our brain in the making of slips on the eve of examination night instead to learn by heart. When we come out of our house, for our career, professional life we do the same, in our office, by not doing work on time, by taking due advantage while submitting of expenses, like fare, medical or any other. We sell ourselves everyday for a few pennies. Don't you think it's true?

We fabricate everything to get maximum gains in our business. We start our business to develop ourselves and to take care of our people, who are associated with us. But we do our work in illusion by not filing proper taxes, which is mandatory, not giving shares to our employees, which is their right. If you have thought of your tomorrow in your today, you will definitely not put yourself in any problem by cheating. Cheaters won't live a long life. You also know this but still. Isn't so?

You will have to do maximum labour, if your principles are clear otherwise you know from your heart, to hide something, you have to do maximum labour. Living a simple, healthy and a well-planned life won't have much problems instead of the life comprising, cheating, which is full of problems and heading towards the premature death of your soul.

Living a full life with a happy ending is a dream of many but only few avail this. We should put ourselves in the least of the problems, by not cheating others because the life for which, we are doing so, will cheat us one day. Then for what, we are cheating, we are not clear. When life cheats, it means death and that is final and forever. We don't get the next chance for the second, to even say sorry for our mistake. So, we have to think, if nothing is permanent, neither the life then what for, we are doing so. You should be transparent that anyone can read you and make a right opinion for you. Sometimes, we know from our heart that this is wrong, but still we do so and then we feel sorry when we see the result. Why so? It's tough to opt for a good path because it is tougher at the start, when there was a way available for you as a shortcut, as a trick, with plus and minus, which could lead you behind the bars. But still we do so. This shows our foolishness that we know at our start, what would be our end, but still, we stick to it.

We won't have answers at the end because we knew of it at the start, at the beginning the path we have opted had never had a happy ending. Try to live your one life with healthy senses that you will never cheat yourself by cheating others.

Just become fair in your work, you will find you are glowing and people around you, have also brightened up with your ray. They will never abuse you even in their dreams and you will live in their hearts.

18

Corruption

You won't find a good soul in the person involved in this. Having no sense, no values and no ethics is the clear meaning of this word. Because values of life won't pay you much, this is what the corrupted man thinks.

They can go to any extent to spoil their soul, they feel happy about themselves that living a corrupted life, with full of money, will give them a standing in the life, they adopt every malpractice to get more and they do so, without thinking.

A simple and straight work through a corrupted hand becomes tedious and cumbersome. A genuine fee of few hundreds converted into few thousands, through a corrupted hand. You can get your work done, while sleeping at your home, through a corrupted hand. These are the few qualities of this personality, whom we say as corrupt.

What makes us corrupt? We know it is the desire of everyone to get more money. But we are also equally responsible today because we don't want to stop them, in their intention, we don't want any delay in our work and sometimes, this also makes a person greedy for money and makes him corrupt.

When we first took bribes, we think in our heart, in our soul and we think for the last also because, after that we don't have a soul, to think upon. We feel happy, when our work, which was pending on the table of a clerk, got done after pursuing and investing. We don't want to fight; neither have we wanted to highlight the problem, which we were facing due to him. We could be resourceful to pay his demand, but what about the person, who does not have the money to pay him.

We have not solved our problem but increased the problems of others. We, ourselves are responsible for this problem, we create it, develop it but never try to resolve it because, we don't want to fight with the prevailing system, but we do want to be the part of the system. If we come out of our shell, we will definitely find it is reduced from our society, system.

To remove a corrupt officer or to transfer him is a tough job than to do with an honest man, because in a web of corruption, it's very difficult to remove one. You have to crush the system by a hard law, so that, the person who breaks the law finds himself broken by the law. Until he fears to do so, you won't be able to get the result from the law.

We make law, we break law and then why do we make it, just to prove that, to run a system, there must be a guideline to run the show, but its weakness is more or less our responsibility. If you feel fear, you will never put yourself near any crime, corruption; otherwise, most corruption is due to one's daredevil nature.

Few intellectual people make the law, but many break so. They feel pride of doing so; don't feel afraid of anything because it is our weakness of law that we always leave loopholes to provoke them to do so. If they feel that taking the law, in the wrong direction, could burn them, and they will have no excuse, they will put themselves away from crime.

You will find hardly a place where there is no corruption, malpractice, because again, its desire of money, to make yourself powerful, to prove yourself wealthy and to feel that possibly, you won't live happily in a simple living, with full of meaning and caring for others.

To break the system of corruption, we require a hard stringent law and your will to fight against it. If you will fight today, others will definitely support you tomorrow, because tomorrow it's their chance to be crushed by corruption. So, make it your first priority to remove this from your society and give a healthy atmosphere to everybody.

19

Character

This is the most important quality of the person, which glows like a gem from his personality. A man with a good character man is different in his perception, in his thought from others, which makes him different in his approach. It's very hard to maintain yourself with this quality and it's very easy to adopt a bad character. "But you will always find yourself good with a good liking from the mass".

It took years to do so, but it took seconds, to get it destroyed in the eyes of someone. Who had a good liking for you, for your behaviour, concept, perception and love? Don't you think so; it is very embarrassed for us, when someone started disliking us, who loved us earlier.

It took years for a tree to develop from a small sapling, same as a character of a person. It was an effort of your family, parents, teachers, friends, your love and finally you, yourself in the making of so, from your childhood to your age at which, you should have that quality to live a healthy life, so, why and what for, you thought to lose it and for the sake of what? You cannot buy the character of the person but you can buy the person because qualities cannot sell, you know this.

We have been given a good quality by the Almighty to forget our past. If we don't have this quality then it will become hard to live. But you should have the quality of a snake and a dog, in you, in your character, because as a snake, never forget his enemies to take revenge and a dog never forgets his master, his well-wisher. The Quality of a snake makes you alert, from your enemy and a quality of a dog, will make you to do a service for your associates. Never forget the two and go ahead with your efforts. Making mistakes are in the human nature, in your life, in your work, in your decision, planning and result. It is not at all necessary to do mistake first and then learn from it, as we say that we should learn from our mistakes, but we could save ourselves from committing the mistakes, by learning from others mistakes, others problems. Do make yourself aware, what's going around you? Why people are in problem? If today they are, tomorrow you could be. So, why don't you, make yourself prepared for it with the answer.

Good and bad experiences both have an equal share in the making of life better. From the good experiences of someone, you will always make your life better but from the bad experiences of someone, you will again save yourself from committing a mistake in your life. So, do understand the problems and the facts of others life and take an example of them in your life, to save yourself and to make yourself.

Try to become a good example to others and make yourself aware of the bad too. Your character and nature are valuable assets of your life and with the two, you will glow like a sun, shine like a moon. So, maintain them and feel the differences from your heart and soul that you are happy and you don't feel regret of having a good character. If you will lose it, you will lose yourself, then for whom you are losing so. Stick to it, like anything, till your end, you will never feel ashamed of yourself and beautify your heart for yourself and others.

Having a good heart, a good character, you will associate to many in your life, but you won't have a single good person with you, if you possess a bad one. So, why don't you prefer to live in a family of good people? Where you can tell or they will understand the meaning of caring, sharing, pairing and the meaning of tears you shed. Living only one life, full of meaning, is to be understood by you, for your sake.

20

Profession

Always love your work, profession and then you won't have to work, till the end of the life. When we got admitted in a professional college, like medical, engineering, law and any design center, we feel great about ourselves, with our hard labour to crack the competition. We celebrate our result, for getting admission but then we forget the ethics or the meaning of that study.

Getting a medical, engineering or law degree won't make you a good human being, until you understand your profession that, you have to serve, with your knowledge. We forget everything, the oath, the dignity of the profession and we forget ourselves too, when we use our knowledge for a bad, and a wrong purpose.

We had not been taught to do so but still we do so. This shows our purpose to opt; a career to serve the person in pain was meaningless.

Only a few colleges have a brand name, status

as reputed and only a few of the students get the value of the course. We all have the same degrees but have different meaning, while we start our practice, professional life. Faculty and student make a college reputed. Funds and management makes a good infrastructure. Quality and dignity makes a course valuable.

We certainly find that the third division and a distinction holder had a different approach and henceforth the result, but they both had the same environment to practice. A doctor feels free to experiment on the life of a poor, an Engineer with no concept in his mind, design, and supervise the foundation of the building. They don't feel fear of anything, because of their poor degree. But what was the mistake of that poor person, who had come to be examined by you, after looking at your degree, your profession. You killed him because of your poor knowledge on the subject. You should have no right to get into the practice, where people take you as a life saviour and you prove to be his murderer.

Very few got this opportunity, to which general masses give respect, because of their profession. So, make yourself clear at the time of joining the course, at the time of attending lectures, at the college, that tomorrow, you have to stand in front of a dying person to save him from his death and you have to prove that the Almighty has given you, knowledge, power to cure the person in need. Do not compromise

in your profession; be efficient with sufficient knowledge, to take care of it.

21

Innovation

Innovation shows your creativity to live a healthy life, prosperous and complete. If we don't feel the need of anything, we don't search for that something. That search makes us creator. It should be for you, for someone else or for the general masses but if you have decided to search for it, you will definitely find it one day.

Living a routine life, with having no charm is nothing more than death. You can carve yourself by searching for your happiness with your innovations. When you will succeed, you'll find yourself, to be the happiest person on this earth. It's true, we never think until we face a problem, but if we have fallen into it, it's good to know its depth and to absorb it, so that it never arises again, in your life.

Innovations and problems have in depth relation with each other, if we won't have a problem, why do we innovate. Need makes our brain unstable and keep on searching for its solution and until we get it, we find ourselves puzzled. If we don't feel needy of anything or rather satisfied with the prevailing atmosphere, environment, we will find ourselves confined in our ideas, approach. Sometimes need makes you fight with your problem for the solution. Needs are the necessity of the life to live it better, so, don't be afraid with your need. Think happy that you have a reason to live, to get it in your life.

22

Book

The Book is a beautiful gift, given by an intellectual person, by writing the values of life, his experience and knowledge for you, to make you complete in your endeavour. It is the valuable asset for you because you are incomplete without it and you will shine, by the knowledge of it. You can make your dream true, if you understand the meaning of it, in your life. We have to love them, care them, save them to make ourselves complete, because of them. You have to understand the meaning of every word clearly because each word has a definition, the relation with your practical approach and result. When you find yourself failing in your effort, this shows, you might have taken something as understood or assumption. Words can make you and destroy you too.

With words we make a sentence, from the sentence, a paragraph, then a chapter and finally a book. It has a relation and every word has its importance in the meaning of the book. From the experience of someone, you can get the solution of your problem. So, believe in the ethics of a book and spend your leisure time with some good books. In the company of idiots you will be called so, but having precious views by reading a book, would put you in the company of intellectuals. You will be happy to understand the problem and having the solutions too. Investing in books shows that how much you love yourself. Clearing of fundamentals, basics, shows, you want a complete definition and nothing as understood. Your investments on the books will prove you, that you know the value of money and its importance that where to invest it, for its maximum return tomorrow. Until you invest today, you won't get a return tomorrow. So, believe that the book can make you an icon tomorrow. Keep on learning till the end of your life because nobody is complete. You can even learn from your junior, if you want to develop yourself. We should believe that with every start of the day, we would exercise our brain and brawn to make ourselves complete, till our end.

Our ego does not want us to come out of our shell and learn from our employee, for our interest and for a good result. The day you will change your attitude and start learning, you will find, you know the answers to many questions now. Why we feel ashamed of asking, if you don't know, sometimes an idiot can ask you a better question than a wise man's answer, so, believe in the principle of learning with every start of a new day and feel them, if you want to learn. You will become complete one day.

23

Law

It's very hard to believe that we have the guideline to run and maintain the society but still we find crime, corruption, cheating everywhere. People are not afraid to break the law and they feel happy of the lacuna of the system. They dare to do crime and we feel ashamed on the dignity of law.

What is the need to make law, if it is to be broken? We just want to give answers to the masses and that's the reason we amend the grasp of law, on the crime. Culprits at the time of doing the crime, never think of the result, its outcome or he won't have that thought committing crime? But he is sure that the complexity in the system would let him free, one day. But the poor chap, whom he killed, the innocent person is died and we forget the incident and start waiting for something new, to happen.

We find a law is there in the court, to discuss, appeal and giving judgment, but we don't find law in our day-to-day life where we are busy in the killing of ethics for our interest. We have defined law elaborately but still, we could not give right judgment, at the right time.

People are puzzled by so, but to whom do they complain, to you, to me or to the system. Plenty of cases are pending in the court, a novice lawyer with a pair of clothes, is now coming in a luxury car having a handsome bank balance from his profession but an innocent man had lost his values on the law.

The Principles are bought or sold every day and a person, who assumes himself wise and shows or rather proves his stupidity, buys it. The Law is there to take care of you, to work in a system, having a policy, for the sake a better life. Do understand the meaning of it, give respect to it and believe in a system that is transparent for all with effective judgment, in the list of hearings.

People are not interested to wind up their job and the result is, we have a person, who has lost faith in the law and the judgment. Judges get their salary, advocates get their fees, but the victim won't get his judgment from the court. They are not bound by any law, but a victim expects fast judgment from them, to save his life from death.

He cannot complain to you, for your lethargic move or the undefined approach to define the procedure, to give judgment. You have to come out of this, to prove that, your interest will be saved from the killers and there is a defined system with less complexity, in which, we are there to work, to analyze, the person in the least time with maximum effort and there is a judgment to punish him, to make him think, again that he will not repeat this again.

A good judgment won't give you, a result, in your approach to change a person, in his personality. You will find another person tomorrow in the court, so, make him think and the masses, that, a crime would lead him to face you and you are not going to save him. You will make him think again and again in the rest of his life that why he did so? And feel guilty of it. You have to become hard from your heart while giving the judgment of death, to save many from that animal, in the shape of a human being.

The Criminal has half developed brain or thought, they don't think, why do they do so? But they do think how to do it? If they can think of this, then why don't you think to give them the best of your knowledge, the most suitable judgment. It is our weakness, our halfhearted approach, that's the reason, people feel free to abuse the law and slap us, by committing the crime. He knows we are not clear, about the definition of law and we find ourselves helpless in the complexity.

It's hard to kill our system, than to kill ourselves and that's the reason, we find ourselves addicts of it, we don't hear a blow, from crime but we keep on, attending the hearing at the court.

We have to develop confidence in the masses that, the law is made for you, to take care of you and to tell the criminals that, you too will be taken care of, if you will play with it. Make a foolproof system, define the meaning of the law, first to yourself and do feel the pain of the person, suffering because of your lethargic move.

You have to assign time for everything, because time has the essence, meaning with the judgment, otherwise tomorrow it would be too late, with the judgment. You too feel guilty, when you will find that the victim is no more. Very few of us have confidence in the system, the defined law; otherwise we are waiting for our number, to be crushed by it, one day. Do kill the lethargic approach, the delay in taking action and develop confidence in the masses that, you will define the law again, solve the pending cases in the court and give guidance to the innocent to save themselves from the hands of evil.

We have to come out of our shell that we are here to work, to justify our soul that we do make ourselves clear that, nobody is dying because of me, for not doing my work, at the right time. We have to make ourselves answerable to us that, before we go to sleep, we will try to clear the pending task. If we will sleep on the files, cases in the day and at night, as we do. I will say you are in dead mode. Come out of it, before it becomes too late.

24

Jealous

The word itself creates a noise in the ears, something negative in the heart and brain, for someone, whom we know and associated with us. Why do we feel jealous? Is it necessity to feel jealous or it is something else. What do we get for being jealous of someone on his result, his achievement? Nothing, simply nothing but we do burn our precious blood by doing so, we kill ourselves, our health, our heart, our good brain by feeling jealous. Don't you find foolishness on our part, that we will get nothing but we will definitely lose something by doing so, but still we adhere to it? What for?

If you will not get anything out of it, it's better to avoid it, as a good businessman or the person having an intellectual brain, who never put his efforts on the job from which he will not get anything. This is also the fact that we feel jealous of those whom we know in our lives, not for those, who are strangers. It's a unique quality of our personality. We find it everywhere, in our studies, work, result, achievements and friendship, love, affection and many more. I think there could be hardly be a field in which we cannot feel jealous for someone. It's hard to fight with it, but you have to, if you believe in the simplicity of the life.

"Few people are preparing for a competition in a hostel building. After a hard labour for one year, few got selected and few dropped. Two lobbies were made at the hostel of selected and dropped. People from the dropped lobby become jealous because they have to prepare now for the second time, but what were the mistakes of those, on being selected in first attempt and known to you, living with you, for a one complete year, as your neighbour, in the hostel". Developing of ill feeling won't give you anything but thinking with a positive attitude that, among the many candidates from all parts of the country, whom you don't know, few are known to you, as your past friend and you were close to him while studying, preparing and tomorrow, if at all you won't be able to clear the exam but still few of your good friends are there at a reputed post to take care of you, to help you in your need.

Never allow developing this complexity in your nature otherwise you will never gain anything instead of losing everything. Feeling inferior won't give any solution to you. You could be bad in many but still you would have at least one good quality and to find it, is the reason of living, your life. Don't feel puzzled with your demerits; don't be feeling ashamed of your failures in the life. But with every failure, try to concentrate on your weakness and again hit for the goal. If you will feel inferior, you will remain inferior, so feel something else, the Almighty has given this sense to you, to judge you that you too have something unique, being provided as a gift by him, to you but you yourself have to find it, search it.

If you have lost yourself then you yourself have to find it too. Sometimes after our many efforts, we won't get results, at that moment you could think like that. He; the Almighty might have thought something else for you or rather wanted to save you from the bad circumstances in the future. Do believe in Him and in you then you won't have to develop any ill feelings in yourself and you will always achieve your goal and the support of the masses. You are not the only one who is fighting with a problem but you are among many, who have lost themselves in the crowd, in the fighting for the more, in the instability of the brain and you have forgotten that the meaning of life is something else and not this. What we are doing and engaged with?

25

Inspiration

It is the power, energy, feeling which we get from some source, which we assume as our ideal. It makes us energized to believe that we can also fight for the betterment of our lives. It gives a meaning to our effort, with an example, as a source and energy.

This is also a fact that, we feel inspired of only living things, which has motion, life and not static one. Its nature to fight and to prove its caliber makes us close to its qualities and we make it, our source of inspiration to change ourselves, accordingly.

It's good to have someone, as your ideal because, then you will try to change yourself according to him and make yourself complete, for your need. It makes us fight for our rights, for our betterment.

You could be inspired by anything, which is there in the nature, and has a life. "I want to prove myself a fool, to learn from the master", because you cannot learn from a person, or he will not teach you, if you prove yourself experienced, until you prove yourself a novice, he will not feel comfortable to guide you, according to his capacity. There wouldn't be clash in the opinion because there is only one master and you are his student. You can learn a lot, if you believe in this principle, otherwise he wouldn't assume you, as his student.

It is the quality of the master that he wants to give, his knowledge, with his satisfaction and he discusses with his students, to make them comfortable with the subject and its meaning.

To make you complete, you have to make yourself transparent, so that you can judge, decide and feel that, why are you lacking? If you are able to know the meaning of your question then you can see, your goal is visible to you. If there is someone, whom you feel could be your source of inspiration, to make your life better then stick to him, till you feel, you have his qualities now. You will be happy to feel him, in your heart and it energizes you, with every endeavour. You will feel yourself in the shelter of that personality, if you are inspired by him, his views, his style to fight, and his way to think with the problem it makes you bold to act and to fight with your comfort.

You won't feel alone in your battle because his presence, in your heart, in your dedication makes you strong that you know your weakness and now you can defend yourself with your clarity of thoughts. It is the part of the life, to give the meaning to life, for the betterment of life, so, if you want to change your life, you have to change your thinking and try to give answers to yourself then you won't live in illusion. You could be inspired by anything or everything but never forget that, it should be able to give meaning to life.

26

State of Mind

It's difficult to describe the mind, its power of understanding, capabilities, abilities and it is hard to determine, what is going on in the mind. Your thinking has a relation with your mind or you can say, your tool of thinking is your mind.

We all know that our brain has a power to think, but still we find sometimes, we are thinking from our heart because of emotions and affections and feel the result, which we have not thought of.

Your heart has no relation with your thinking but still, you find a person to be good at heart while giving him work and compromise with the result. Knowingly, you are responsible for your ill fate and your condition. No doubt, your heart has a relation in your thinking, to give a soft touch to your decision from the mind, but you keep its limitation, in your decisions to make you a good decisive person.

You won't gain, if you think from your heart, so it's good to make relation from your heart, but how good is your relation, is the job of your mind, your brain. In most of the cases, when you find yourself in a problem, you would definitely think that, it is because of your thinking from the heart, instead of your mind.

The two has have different field to work, but has a relation too, to make your decision healthy, wise and intelligent. You will never fail, if you think of your mind but your relations make your heart think also.

You cannot discard this fact knowingly, you sometimes compromise, because of your heart's decision and your hard decision of your mind becomes secondary. You are responsible for your mistake then; because your mind had made you alert that you could be wrong. Instead if you believe whole-heartedly from your heart, to think from your mind, what is the best decision for you, to make of you a complete person?

It's difficult to judge the stage and the state of the mind of a person. A half developed or undeveloped brain would not give you any result or rather make your brain dirty too. No need to involve yourself with a person having an underdeveloped brain, if you find him in the developing stage. He will not understand you or your approach and thoughts and he will consider you, as a fool. You have to smile at him, on finding him at his stage of development. No need to discuss anything, your exercise will become futile and you will find yourself ashamed that why you tried to convince him.

Discussion with a person having a healthy brain would lead you to a solution or conclusion; otherwise, you will find yourself in a problem. So, before you start your effort, do judge the level, state and stage of his mind, otherwise, only listen to him, give a smile but don't reply. Sometimes listening is the best solution, to make you happy forever.

27

Interaction

The best way to develop yourself and to know your weakness, you have to interact with people. The more you interact, the more you become confident, to express yourself, to understand where are you lacking?

Whenever you go to a meeting, do prepare yourself with it, the issues, and topics to be discussed and also try to know about the person with whom you are going to discuss. This way you will become more clear and confident while discussing.

Your homework will prove something better with your class work at the time of discussion and you will be able to come to a conclusion with your effort. If you will study about the person, his attitude, weakness, likings and his interests, it will make you easy to prepare a rough profile of his personality and this exercise will help you understand him, prior to the meeting and at the time of the meeting, you will find that you are not talking with a stranger.

It will make it easy to make him understand your feelings, views without any difficulty. An incomplete exercise won't gain you a favourable result, so be prepared for everything, so that you won't fail, in your effort.

"I wanted to be the best man for him at the time of interaction and for that, I have to do some homework, to make me feel that I am presentable now, and I know about him, too."

28

Personality

Personality, this is the quality of the person by virtue of which he can differentiate himself, from others. We want to put less effort, in building it and that's the reason, we find ourselves in the mass. You have to define yourself to you, to make yourself presentable, in front of others and make them feel that you are different from others.

It counts everything your voice clarity, confidence, trait, dress, body, attitude, attention, punctuality and your approach and many more; you will find that you are glowing. To put yourself in a good personality mould, to make yourself complete and presentable you have to understand what you are lagging in. What makes you common among others?

It's good to copy a good personality to make yourself complete because, you have found something incomplete in you and you have your full right to make yourself complete. Living in the present day it is the need of the system that you try for the best for yourself. Adopting the way, the others do, won't give you a good personality but shows obscenity from your clothes, thought and your approach. Sometimes knowingly or unknowingly we are responsible for our mishappening, because we adopt the trend without realizing its outcome. It's good to move to the present but simultaneously take care of your future. Everybody wants to become famous in this world, for name and fame, and they can go to any extent. A film actress can drop her last cloth, to get the fame, in the media, mass, with the movie, irrespective of thinking, that her approach could lead to a bad example in the society, and destroy the dignity of the women. But they want popularity and money, and for the two, they can drop anything.

Setting a bad example with your profile in the media could crumble the system and we find a rise in the number of rape, sexual assault and molestation. Understanding the meaning of these words is different but feeling the pain of these acts on the victim is entirely different. Nobody can feel the pain of the victims, except the victim herself. For them, it might be the joy for a few minutes but for the victim, it was the pain, for her entire life.

She cannot face herself in front of the mirror and you are responsible for that, to provoke them in your bare act. For you, it was an act but for someone, it was a horrific experience. The general mass assumes you to be his or her inspiration, so, try to give them the real story, the fact and make them aware that getting a good entertainment from a bad movie, would lead you in a problem, in the real world.

You don't have any right to kill them, by your bare act and thoughts. So, make yourself clean and give them healthy relations and thoughts. You are more or less also responsible for your result because, you live in the illusion and want to be in illusion until something does wrong with you.

Crying on your mishappening is feeling ashamed of yourself that, why you had not thought with complete meaning. Partial knowledge of anything is always dangerous and all that glitters is not gold. We all know the meaning of it, but still we behave or think like a fool.

We always like those things to see, which we cannot see easily and that is the reason, we want to get entertainment, something different from the routine. Don't you think we are responsible for it because, it was our interest which was the reason, we find, that they want to show. You have to admit that, if you would not accept it, they won't make it, your interest makes them to do so and you are more or less responsible for your thinking.

You have to save yourself with your clear thoughts and likings so that you won't believe in cheap stuff and you want to breathe fresh air, to make yourself happy, till your end. An incomplete entertainment with no values is a poison for your life and you won't survive for long if you continue it. Do understand the meaning of all and make yourself clear with everything.

29

Writing

You can know the quality of the person through his writing and his signature such as his perception, character, expression and clarity of his thoughts and likings. Good writing makes it easy to read your expression, your views and it makes a sense in your part also because you have devoted your time, in making yourself clear with your expression for others. Persons who are in a hurry to get results from his work, we usually find illegible writing and his personality reflects from it.

As clarity of ideas can be judged from your uninterrupted speech, clarity of your writing shows how systematic and defined you are with your profile. Your signature also has links to your personality; it shows creativity, nature and confidence.

Define yourself with your writing so beautifully that everybody finds a person in you, as having a good heart, a good soul. If you do not have the quality to hide anything, conceal anything and believe in transparency than your words, your writing should have the brightness of fact and you should hate to see untidy work. All the good thoughts in which we find the meaning of life, love and faith are written in the spirit of good words, in good writing and make us feel that expression of beautiful feelings do require a platform of good writing as a medium in the transferring of thoughts from the brain to the paper.

30

Motivation

it's a tough job to motivate someone, to make him feel about his power, his strength. You have to involve yourself with him and to feel yourself in his mould of thinking and find out his problem, his desire and why he thinks that he cannot.

it's true, giving an advice is an easier work than to work with that advice. If you will not feel yourself competitive, then you will not fight with your full extent and finding your power to express your effort, for your target is again finding yourself that, you can win; perhaps you know your limits but you also must know how to win? It is not a hard task to find your limitation until you listen to yourself, judge yourself and find yourself. It is our foolishness that we want to see the mirror for our beauty and not to find someone, who is living there in your heart as a good or a bad identity. If you make yourself answerable to you, then you will work for yourself, because you don't want to make yourself a fool and if at all you will not clarify yourself, you will prove so, at your end. Giving advice, lecture has no meaning until you make them feel that their limitation of thinking makes them to listen you, otherwise they too are well capable to give advice. There is nothing as special in me as compare to you, the only difference, I can think and now it's your turn to do so, for yourself, for the betterment of your life.

You are not having your success because you have not thought of it, properly. "If you want to see change in your life, you have to change your thinking", so, don't you think, this is the only tool by which, you can make yourself. Don't wait for the help, from someone, till it becomes late for you to help yourself, just find your abilities and put your brain and brawn to implement it, you will find yourself happy, with your effort.

"Opportunity never comes to those who wait, they are captured by those, who dare to attack," is a very right statement, waiting for your chance is good if you are in a queue and otherwise you just have to wait for the result of your effort and nothing else.

Sometimes you have to make opportunity in your favor, by pursuing and it's not bad to say, "Pursuit of success should be endless". You have to make every opportunity as your chance, provided to you, for your development and if you compromise by not availing it, you will just prove to be a loser. You don't know at which opportunity you are going to crack success for yourself and by losing your chance, this could be possible, you won't get it again. It's good to clap for the racers, but I will prefer to run in the race and make the public to clap for me too. It's immaterial whether I come first or last, but it matters if you are in the game, in the race and not in the crowd. The reason for being in the race was, you have known your capabilities and now you cannot put yourself waiting for your opportunity.

Very few people have this power to express themselves in the public, to let them know that you know your power and now it's your turn. A dying person in the hospital, on the bed or a patient in coma knows this thing or feels death breathing at his side every moment. With your effort and your love, you can make him feel that the cycle of life has a phase of death also and it's a bitter fact, to be felt and experienced by everyone, who is living and you have to believe that whosoever, who has come in this world, has to go one day and nobody can tell, when and how? It's a mystery, but it's a fact. You can make a patient rejuvenate, if you can develop an interest in him and the power to live and to fight with his illness. Your will is the most powerful medicine, you will have it till your last breath; you will not lose it, anyway. Your endless effort can bring a patient back from coma, if you keep on whispering in his ears, that, he is the most important person in your life and you will become alone if he does not listen you. Your effort will give you a gain, in shape of him and you will never feel pain for your effort, when he was in bed.

If it is sure you cannot save him then its better to believe, first in your heart that you will make him believe that, he has lived his life, beautifully and this is the time to satisfy yourself with your efforts and your fights that you have been given only these years, to do so and you have done your duty to your satisfaction.

This could be possible, you feel puzzled with your left out duties, your responsibilities, but now it is not in your hands, otherwise you would have been given some more time, by Him.

Believe in yourself at the stage and the age, that you want to live your every minute of your one life, so that, you won't feel at the time of going that something has been left or missed. To be a motivator, you have to be very powerful from your heart, your sense and your brain because you have to feel the problem from all the three. Every person has good and bad qualities in him/her and it is a fact that we forget his best remarks, which is in many numbers but we never forget to scold him for his bad remark. It's a human psychology that we forget the good one easily but we never forget the wrong, but this shows your selfishness because he is also a human being and it's a property of this creature that a sensible man does not want to commit mistake knowingly, his remark could be the phase through which he could not able to judge, his wrong words. So, make yourself sensible to feel and make him feel the same, because you cannot be a sensible person alone, if you want to have a healthy relation with him. We all know that when we take medicine, in our illness, it makes us healthy with its action, when we listen some soothing music, it gives coolness to our mind but when we to hear something harsh, it gives us an unpleasant headache.

Motivations do have the same action as others but it is also temporary, because until you feel that you know your power and understand the vacuum of your life, you will find yourself complete and feel the effect, till the end. It could be anything that motivates you, you can have a lesson from an ant that how she can kill an elephant, who is much bigger than her, in every way, but still, it's good to have good thoughts and good examples to make you feel revived, for your best effort and this makes you feel energized that you have regained your lost faith in yourself. That would be the brightest day of your life when you will find your own drawbacks and cut them from the root. If you will not find them and live with them, you won't live healthy and differences will definitely come up in your life. It's hard to listen to or face our drawbacks because we don't want to believe that we are incomplete, yet, and we want to keep on living in the same mould. If you will not come out of this stupidity, I can only say that you will not able to face the eyes of death with confidence.

31

Patience

It shows your level of maturity and how do you react, with your senses at the time of a problem. Maturity does come from knowledge and experience but patience shows that your maturity has attained that level at which you have known, when to react and how to react? Patience is the power of the person to make him feel that, he will not break his silence before time.

Impatience shows your immaturity that you won't believe in your capabilities and that's the reason, you seem to be a confused person. Patience proves you with your result that you knew that you wouldn't face failure after your effort and it pays you with your satisfaction and calmness in your mind.

Your excitement makes you lose your patience. It's a fact, if you don't feel excited, you won't believe in youth because the excitement and youth have a relation, as patience and maturity have. You cannot suppress your excitement for your patience; both have different impact in your life, importance in your life because it makes you feel, with your effort, to know, where you stand and with time, it makes you more excited to break your patience for the result.

Believe in the principle of patience that it will definitely come to you, if you will not lose your heart and interest. Prove your maturity by being patient and break the silence at the proper time.

32

Comfort

You have your every right to make yourself comfortable for the betterment of your life and if you compromise, you will always be a loser. If you are puzzled because of something or someone and that gives you a headache and you are avoiding to taking a better decision, for the time being then again, you won't feel comfortable for long.

Things which you are good at and feel good to do them, then you must do that thing, irrespective of other hindrances. You won't feel yourself cheated then, because it was your liking, your interest and this is a psychological fact that we do the work we are interested in, from our heart and with full enthusiasm.

With your enthusiasm and your interest, you will definitely have a better result, of your effort and you will find yourself involved to its roots, with your interest.

"I don't go there, where I feel myself surrounded with problems and with a headache but I prefer to go there, where I find myself, part of them, of their healthy discussion for the betterment of our life."

If any of the chords is not tuned, then you will never hear the soothing music and you have to change it to feel better, otherwise being in a depression, you won't live for long, your own state of mind will kill you.

So, to make yourself comfortable, you have to reduce your problems to feel you have understood the effect and now you will not compromise.

33

Music

It makes me feel good when I hear it. I feel revived, when I understand, the meaning of it. It makes me flow like a river; it fills the loneliness of my life and becomes my companion, when I feel sad and alone. It fills the voids of my life and makes me feel that I am incomplete, without it.

You can change the interest of the person, mood of the person and recuperate him from his illness with the effect of music. Life without music is just as life without colors, you will definitely feel something is missing in your life, if you believe that, as there are seven colors in the rainbow and there are seven tones in the music too. It shows the relation of the color with the music and it has a sense with life too, with the two.

It is the medicine to revive your life, to make your brain and heart feel good and happy. You want to listen to something fast, exciting when you are happy and slow, soothing when you are sad. This shows the phase, your reaction and your liking with your mood. You and your favorite music can travel for long, drive for long and it reduces the exertion from the journey. This shows the fulfillment of music in our life and how we are dependent on it, for the changing of our mood, phase of our life, and state of our mind and are feel, we are incomplete without it.

34

Time

It is the essence of your life, to make your life beautiful, planned and systematic. If you will love to be on time, you will find time will give you ample opportunities to complete yourself. You have to define it, for your life, by yourself that how much important is time in your life?

You have to plan your schedule, to make you aware that, you cannot stop the time. It will not stop for you, it will make you, a past, a failure, if you will not understand the importance of time in your life, with your work and your schedule.

Planning and programming are the essence to make your schedule defined; otherwise you will be late in your result. You have to calculate your efficiency and dedication before you hit the target so that it won't rebound back to you, for a second attempt. It should go in the hole of success.

The time machine never fails; it calculates your effort and gives you, your result at your time, if you are sure about yourself and your work. You will feel satisfied, if you work according to your plan, you won't have different results that do not match your desires and expectations.

If you know the value of time, you will try to define your work, complete your work, within your time, so, you won't feel ashamed of yourself for killing valuable time. Because of our immaturity and wrong policy, we find ourselves in problem and tension, when we execute our work, at the eleventh hour.

We are never sure about its working and completion because, we won't have proper time to give it the best shape. We find ourselves in a hurry, with the completion and by mistake, we make a blunder. You are responsible for it, because you made the essence of the time meaningless, when you have enough time to make it, plan it and proceed with it. You have your choice in your hand, to feel the difference because you won't get this time again. Utilize it, with your maximum effort so that you feel happy that, you know the result and you are happy with it.

Your endeavour to make your life complete has a relation with your time too. You won't get another opportunity for the time you lost, so, don't take chances to lose time.

The definition of time is to be understood, so that you won't fail in proper planning of time. Successful persons know the value of time, and they cannot compromise with anything for a time. You cannot recover your loss, if do not feel the importance of time. It's a fact that you will die one day and your life cycle would end there, with your death. So, believe in the cycle of life and that life is important with time, as both the things are running, but at your death you won't be able to see the next moment. Believe in the principle of time and the cycle of life to make yourself complete.

35

Management

It has a key role in the development of your personality and your status. If you are clear with the definition, you won't take chances without proper planning. Management increases the productivity through technical innovations taking into account human factors. You have to believe in the person and craft his skills to make yourself benefited.

You have to plan with him, the policy and procedures and adhere with time management, for a productive result. It has a strong grasp on the industry, without it, you cannot maintain the job for a long.

A good manager is strong enough to run the company, despite of his lack of knowledge in the technical matters. You would have found that a non-technical person with his management skills is handling the job with technical hands and with satisfactory results. If you are clear with the definition of management, you will find yourself good enough to handle any task.

Knowledge of management makes you, a good director, to direct the manpower, to get the result. This is also a quality that gives you the power, to handle the people for your need and to make them feel that nothing is impossible, if you are on the right track.

Feel yourself complete and make your effort to complete the meaning of teamwork, with the definition of management. Define the principle of work, with your subordinates and make them feel, their responsibilities, duties and correct their approach, to know the status of their brain and clarity with their job.

A good symposium in the interest of the work, would lead you towards your goal. If you are clear with your job, you won't be confused at the time of performing. Do take your time, in clarifying, all the pros and cons related to the job, so that, at the time of performing you won't be confused with your approach.

Planning and scheduling are the stages at which you have your liberty to analyze the best option to perform your work, make yourself aware with all the negativity so that you can prepare yourself with its answer, in advance. You won't get results with your entire endeavour, but you have to make yourself clear that, you will fight with your brain and brawn to complete yourself. Management makes you love and solve the problems and you will feel happy to be a manager.

Quality carves your ability to make your opportunity an impact to get a good shape. Do feel the need of the management in your life; as in your work you will find, you have a clear option to opt without any confusion. The word has a relation with your success, so, define it, for yourself and complete yourself.

36

Precaution

Precaution, prevention, attention makes you vigilant so that you don't get into a problem knowingly. You have been provided senses to examine the circumstances to save yourself from evil, with your knowledge and sometimes experiences gained by someone else. No need to pay for your mistakes willingly; avoid being in problem, if you smell anything wrong.

A good experience makes you decisive, to take a good decision. Precaution, prevention and attention are the stages at which you have not lost anything but you have sufficient time to make yourself aware of the problem. Very few can smell the problem, before falling into it; otherwise we avoid thinking in length, so as to save ourselves from the darkness. Sometimes, we are provided with one or two opportunities to think and a big accident could be avoided, if you could make yourself smart, before it could happen. We fight with our problem, when we fall into it and do feel sometimes, the intuition that we knew, this is going to happen. We became careless and the result is the darkness in our life. If we could have thought earlier, we could have saved our hard earned money and utilized our valuable time in some, positive effort, to make our life bright, but now fighting with the problem, to reduce the darkness from the life, to see a bright sun again, makes us puzzled.

When we fall in into a problem, we see, we have to use everything to get out of it, i.e., time, money, labour, devotion, energy etc. All these things are valuable for us, because it takes time to make it, but we lose them in a day, with an accident. We would have saved them all, if and only if, we would have thought, used our brains, smell the problem at the start. This is the limitation of our brain that we never want to think at the start but we do think at the end, when the problem has come. We feel stressed, when we think which you can see carved on the face of the person but those who do not put themselves in stress, while thinking at the beginning, remains in the stress, till the end of their life. We should never skip these stages, at which, we have ample time to discuss, analyze, to make ourselves clear so that we avoid any unforeseen problems by taking due precaution, prevention and paying attention. We have to put only our brains to work but if you fall in the problem, you have to use everything. So, why don't you give some work to your brain to analyze and come out of this limitation of thinking? The more you use your brain, the more you beautify your life. So, make your life happy, with happy thoughts and careful thinking.

37

Freedom

You cannot understand the meaning of freedom until you assume like or feel like a slave. Somebody is ruling on your head and you have to obey him, entirely. You cannot complain, cannot disobey his orders, and cannot be disheartened, while performing his directions. You have to do, whether you like it or dislike it. Your liking is immaterial to me and you are bound to serve me, till your last drop of blood. Then you feel that you want to know the meaning of freedom. How do you feel, after you get freedom?

We put the beautiful birds in the cage, just to listen to their sweet voice, just to see them in front of our eyes, and we disturb humanity and the nature too. Nature has given them wings to fly and a sweet voice to spread, but you have broken the relation, for your interest and killed the adventurous life of a bird. This is true that we are living in our interest and we die for it, we fight for our interest but we never fight for our right.

To get the work done, to make our interest complete, we associate people with us, for our work but we never make ourselves clear that, he is also like us. He and I could also have the interest, in you, for you, for your work. If one could make him feel that, he will also put his interest to get the work done, then you will find that your work has double the interest and you are going to get a fast result, an accurate result. But we never make an effort to do so.

If you try to develop interest, affection, care in them, for you and your work, you will find teamwork and team spirit has developed and you are not alone to make your dream come true. Don't feel that, they are your slaves and you are their master, things won't run long, if you have this attitude.

You will be killed, with this approach, if you won't change your way of thinking. If you treat them as your part and care for them, in their needs, hear their requirements, suggestions and give them reward for their effort, you will find they are at the right time, in the office. You are having your result in your hand and people are satisfied with the meaning of effort, dedication and caring.

They won't leave you till your end and you won't leave them, in their need. If you both have the clear meaning of freedom and slavery, you will feel, freedom of giving speech, in the interest of the work and appreciation for getting a good result, has made you clear in your thought and you are living in the heart of many.

Everybody seeks appreciation for his efforts, at the result and never forget to give him a big applauds, in the public. You will find many are coming forward, to fight for you, for your work.

38

Prison

The place where we keep a person, confined, out of reach from the world, to make him feel that, we can live without you and we won't live, if you are there, with us.

We put them behind the bars and feel safe, from them. We give a very good judgment, to confine him in a cell, for his entire life and then we never think for him, what has happened to him, is there any change in him, on in his thinking or is he still the same? When a baby was born, he was not a criminal, but he could be the child of a criminal. Environment, circumstances and ill fate lead him to the negative approach. His brain was clear of sins, at the time of birth and you made him complex, with the complexity of life.

When he was a child, you have not thought about him, at his youth as well as, you did not think of him but when he took the negative approach to make his life run, to make himself happy, by doing wrong deeds and then stuck in the quicksand of the crime and caught by you, red-handed, his life took a new turn, because, then you will put your intellectual brain to give him the best judgment in your knowledge.

It was your duty to do so, but it was again your responsibility, to feel that power to give judgment was my duty, but to make a criminal feel that he has done something wrong and that's the reason, he is in front of you, facing his trial, is also the part of the judgment. If you cannot make him think so, your judgment was incomplete and you will find another. Keep on giving judgment without realizing its effects, in total, won't make you a complete person. If you are able to make him think that, he is responsible for his sin, you will find, he is changing and you will feel happy with your efforts. Very few want to put their brain, to become a complete person, from their intellectual brain otherwise we would not have the limitations of crime, neither a criminal. Simply putting them behind the bars won't make any change in them, the day they will complete their sentence; they will adopt the same ways. Do something different with them, so that, they at least think that there is something wrong in them, "Am I responsible for this, can't I live a happy life without it?"

If you make them feel so, you will find we have gained a good momentum in the speedy development of our nation. They are the hurdles in the development and we make ourselves busy for nothing. Remove the problem from its root and make a good foundation, for the development of the nation. This is also a fact that because of his ill brain, a patient won't able to think, analyze, your effort and then, your exercise becomes futile. He will laugh at you and consider you to be a fool; you don't have any work and should just leave him to his opinion. If you find, with your numerous effort he is not able to getting you or think himself to be very smart, give him the right place in the darkness and forget him, on his ending. He won't live long now and save the innocent from him because; it is also your responsibility to give them bright and safe life.

Releasing a criminal because of insufficient evidences, means killing another innocent person. Do try your best, with best of your knowledge that if, he can use his brain, to do a crime, you will use yours to give him the best sentence, to make him feel that he will not repeat it again. If we know that the animal can harm us, we kill it, without thinking about his life, his pain because, we want to live a healthy life, which we won't get again.

Knowingly, we never compromise when our life is concerned; we want hundred percent assurances that we will live, till our end. So, never, compromise with a personality, if he is not clear, in his perception or way of thinking and can harm you. Put him in the darkness because, your life is valuable for everybody.

39

Change

We always feel good, when we find a change in our life. It could be anything in shape of change that is, changing of your profession, place, job, your house, even the orientation of bed with other accessories, to make you feel comfortable for a sound sleep. It could be anything or everything that makes you happy with your change because we want to feel revived in our life, to fight with a better potential and a new enthusiasm.

When we feel uncomfortable with our mood or interest, we want a change of place and that's the reason, we go for a short trip or vacation. Changing of place and a new environment gives a boost to our feelings and heals our pain because staying in an old mould, for long makes us puzzled with our adventurous desire.

This is our psychological weakness that our mind accepts the change as an effort to revive interest. We find ourselves energetic in our effort because our mood, our mind has a liking for change and we always feel good with our action and then result won't be different from our expectation.

We want to live every minute in the changed environment, feeling, place and that makes us feel good and happy with our life. If you want to see change in your life, you have to change your thinking and it is the fact for a bright tomorrow, but you have to change your thinking today. So, come forward and feel the change in your life.

40

Peace

We all want to have this in our life and we do our best to find it, to make our life healthy and in it's search we keep on wandering here and there, to distant places, to make our soul happy and satisfied.

It has a great importance in our life because without it, you cannot do anything. Neither can you think nor can you act and its absence makes you kill yourself. Persons who have peace in their life, you will find them more energetic, dedicated and laborious, because then they have good power to think and express themselves with their effort, in their work.

If you feel calmness in your head, you will find you have power to resolve any crisis or problem; otherwise the lack of peace in your soul would become the problem for others too.

If you believe in the system or working systematically, you will have everything defined, your effort, dedication and the result because then you have peace in your mind to define yourself. We don't have to go anywhere in its search, if we are clear with the ethics, values and principle of life.

Our complexity makes us puzzled, and the result; we disturb our peace of mind. If you remain in this state for long then I can say you won't live long. Make yourself defined and have nothing to hide from yourself and feel from your heart that where you are lacking and leading, then you will know the meaning of system and you will find peace. Persons who are clear with them, they don't feel the need to search for peace because they know the meaning of peace from their heart.

41

Politics

It is the tool by which you can make a nation. Its development more or less depends on the ethics of politics. It is the blood of the nation for making the relation and to define its principle and policies.

Politics is a strategy, to act for the betterment of the nation and its people. The Interest of the masses and the power of the nation, governs the politics. How powerful you are in the making and maintaining the relations, show the clarity and the meaning of politics.

But how do you find yourself in the present scenario of politics and the political parties. You won't find you are having an answer to justify your ground, facts and standing. You are there, but where, that you are not clear with. The reason behind this is the complexity of politics.

The few has defined, for his interest and not in the interest of the nation and the masses. They know your problems, your weakness and they make it to issues in their speech, and they make such a good show that you find yourself with the solution but remain with the problem at the end.

You know the power of yourself that they are because of you and for your problem only. Politics is the knowledge to give direction to your quality of leadership to give the solution to the masses and to make them feel that they are a part of the nation.

Very few have this power to lead a group, to make them stand, to listen to what you are talking about. But we forget the ethics and values of it and make ourselves, the runner of the race, to grasp the power, to become the leader, to make us wealthy, with the public money.

It is the general public, who is being crushed for your need and they lost the confidence in you and feel disgusted that, why they trusted you? You don't have this right to kill the interest of the masses and the faith, with which, they have chosen you, as their leader, to work for their problem and happiness.

You will remain alive in their hearts and never fail in the contest, if you love to solve their problems and hear them. They are your power and you are their leader, so why don't you make them feel proud of their selection.

If you want to live your life, even after your death, live in their heart, you won't die, then. A common man cannot even express himself for his right; he does not even know that what his right is. So, it becomes your duty to oblige them for their support, to make you stand on your feet to fight for them. If you are clear with the values of a common man, you will be a man of the mass. They won't leave you with their support and you won't be happy to find them in problems.

On getting the confidence of the public, it was our duty to feel them confident for their trust and a transparent relation has to be maintained to believe in the values of a common man. Being a common man you are on the verge to face the values of your trust first. So, make yourself intelligent before somebody proves it different.

No need to make you a laughing matter for them but to make them feel that you are the matter of discussion, for your betterment and satisfaction. Knowing of your right makes you capable to feel that you are special for yourself and for them; otherwise you will lose yourself in the crowd. They make use of your confidence and forget their confidence in you and prove that the problem and you are synonymous.

It was your mistake that you have given your confidence for a person, party without knowing the ethics or values. It's difficult to trust but you have to trust someone and make him feel that the value of life is the foundation of every principle.

Simply without analyzing the person, the party and taking decisions in the illusion, is not the solution for your problem but a mistake cause due to your hurry, proves that, you are responsible for your fate.

Leaders who are not clear with themselves but want to come in power, has a different definition of the politics, they want to define it as a trick to be played politely to make fool of the innocents. No need to prove yourself so, but make yourself intelligent that, who is the fool? You are responsible for the development of the nation, to make your country glow in the world map, to make yourself defined for them that you are clear in your perceptions and ethics of the politics.

They speak of us, our problems, differentiate them from others and make ourselves as an issue to discuss, but only at the time of getting confidence. Why so? You have to fight for your right but make them aware that you are not a child and have the sense that is why you are speaking so and for what you recall me now, for your support.

Believe in this, if you are clear with yourself and with the masses, you won't have to please anyone, your quality will make your leader and your effort to listen to them in their need, will make you the winner of their heart.

Never ditch them for their interest and faith otherwise you will become a past, very soon. Very few have this quality and caliber to work in the forefront in the making of the nation, with the satisfaction of the masses.

A good leader makes a country feel proud with its development with the support of the masses, to make them clear that a common man is as important as a special dignitary in the making of the nation.

42

Wise and Fool

Why a wise person, intellectual person wants to give the answer of a good question than a foolish one? To give the reply to a good question, you have to put your brain only, but to reply a foolish question, you have to put two things, your brain and your heart and otherwise you won't reply it. Your heart makes you feel and your brain makes you to judge, the level of the question.

If you want to take something out of a person, his capacity of the brain, his patience, his maturity, ask him a stupid question, you will have the personality of that person, if he replies. If he does not, then he is a self-centered person and cannot be a public personality. Sometimes a fool can ask you, a good question than the wise man's answer. They have different perception, of their personality and their approach.

Fools have a limitation to think or they don't think, they simply act and then react to the failure but the wise have different approaches for their attempt. They don't want to attempt for the second time, so they make themselves clear first, before they start their efforts.

If you have the limitation to think, it shows you love your success least. Between the wise and the fool, there is one thing that is missing, is the tool of thinking. Thinking with a positive attitude makes you wise but fools are programmed to act, to behave that way since they have a void of thinking and they are aware of it.

Winners are said to be wise and losers the fools, because they are different in their approach, clarity and that's the reason, their results are different. How can you win and become wise? You just have to concentrate on your abilities, your power to strike. Your effort will gain momentum, if you are clear from your heart that the procedure, you have adopted to achieve the target is fair and you have understood the meaning of your job.

Wise has the quality to plan everything but the fools have the quantity of mistakes, for them. It is good to learn from the mistakes but there is no need to do mistake first and then learn you can even learn from the mistakes of others. This is a fundamental of life.

Make yourself wise, with your decision and could be the experience of a fool, to make your effort, the best, for the result. Winners are wise because they have a good achievement with them, but losers are fools because they have one more bad experience with them, as a failure.

Everybody has different nature, different character so, you are not the only one, but you are among many, who might have lost the game because of immature planning. With every failure, you make yourself strong for your opponent; very soon, you will be stronger than him. A good planning, a dedicated effort enables you to have a good result and a wise person never compromises with his efforts.

Failure is the part of success; fools do not know the meaning of success. You cannot analyze the extent of happiness at the success, until you have tasted the bitterness of failure. With every failure I think in my mind that I am still incomplete, to get success, to taste the joy, to feel happy with my achievement. But simultaneously, I feel from the core of my heart that I will not feel disgusted but there might be something, still left for me, to meet, to have an experience from its effect to make me, complete for life that is forever.

Wise has patience to wait for the success and fools are the patients of failures. Your patience proves that, you believe in success, in the meaning of a long relation, with this thing clear in my mind that, I do deserve it, to have it for me? Nobody is complete in this world, so we should believe in this ethics that, with every start of the day, we would put our brain and brawn to make our self-complete. You could develop yourself even from your junior if you want to learn. You have to come out of your shell to believe that, you are incomplete. If I have to make myself complete, I will never compromise in learning. You will be happy to have answers of all, because you are not confined in yourself, you know that mind has no limitation, if you want to think, to make yourself complete.

43

Memory

Memory is the quality of the brain to recall the past to make you feel that you have an experience. It is the power of the brain to retrieve, recall from the past to benefit you, for your present.

Every brain has a capacity to recall, we forget sometimes, not able to retrieve and this is also a fact that our brain has a limitation to recall. Its good and its bad also to have a good memory because having a good memory, all the time your past experiences will counteract with your present, and you won't forget the pain, the insult, the humiliation and you will feel destroyed because of it. With your bad memory, you will find yourself in embarrassing situations many times but more so you won't feel pain for long, for your insult.

Time is the factor with which we forget our pain and live happy in the present otherwise we would keep on fighting with our pain and won't live long. Why we forget? The reason for this is, it was not useful for us, might be unnecessary in our schedule or you might have not given importance to it while learning. If you make a relation of an event, person, place or the chapter of your book, your class, lecture anything like a story in a stream, it will take time to forget. Less important or isolate things, which we have taken casually without learning by heart, understanding of mind, its relation, we forget easily.

It's good to have a good memory because it saves you from the repetition of your mistakes and make you aware with your past incidents and bad experiences.

44

Stress

You cannot find yourself for long, if you remain in stress. You are killing yourself slowly with the poison of stress and your death will be caused by it is sure. You know the fact but you find yourself with the same stress.

A person in stress is a patient and you won't find a healthy solution for him. You cannot complete your work to your satisfaction, being in stress, you have to come out of it, to make yourself feel that you feel easy, without it, otherwise your nervous system has a complaint. "Why do you want to kill yourself?"

Your efficiency to do your work also decreases and you won't find yourself with satisfactory results. What makes you work in stress, if you have to do otherwise also? It makes a difference to your results and it affects your personality also. Stress in your work, might be because of your eleventh hour decision or due to your non-punctuality with your schedule. It could also head you to an additional problem and you keep on fighting to cope with it, to save yourself.

Make yourself clear that, if you have to do it, you will do it with cool head otherwise something would be left in your head in a hurry and in stress. You kill your health, you kill your mind and its efficiency and its ideas and you kill others too, with your attitude of being in stress. You have to plan yourself with your work so, that you find yourself easy with the work.

Our brain has a capacity to think and its extent depends upon the personality, the attitude and the way you want yourself. You won't find a healthy solution, if your brain has a limitation to think, because of stress and its deterioration, has a reason that you are not able to recall, retrieve from your past.

The most important and valuable part of your body is your brain or you can say, every part of your body deteriorates, if you put yourself in stress for long. This could be possible that you won't see tomorrow because of stress, by killing your health so, why don't you make yourself believe that an enemy will never carve your life in a better pursuit and that you have only one life to live and you want to avail this chance. Stress has no relation to the development and you will find yourself confined in your thoughts, you won't find yourself dedicated to your work and it will make you puzzled with everything.

Find yourself, define yourself, make yourself clear with your work and judge your effort and take your time to accomplish your task with dedication and interest. You will be happy with your result and find yourself young to tackle any problem, at any stage. With stress you will do only one thing, that too, knowingly, killing yourself, otherwise you have everything healthy, to make you happy with your effort in your work. Without it there is happiness and with it there is not a long time for you to think. So, think again and feel happy for your choice.

45

Crowd

You are highly unsafe if you are in a crowd or mob because you will lose your identity, if you will try to tell them their. It's very hard to disintegrate them, from their nation, for which they have gathered and if you sing anything among them not in tune, they will change your chord first.

A mob wants to listen to that for which they have come to listen, so being in them, never try to make them listen to something else. People hear those whom they feel capable to make them listen and it is also a fact that it's hard to make anybody listen, to you.

Leaders have a power to control them, a singer has a quality to make them silent and isolate themselves in the crowd. It is not the power of everybody to change the direction of thinking,the theme of the crowd; the crowd has no sense, no feelings, if they become violent and at that time, it's tough to make them feel, that they are wrong.

You can make a person feel for his mistake but it's tough to say anything against the crowd. You will find yourself entrapped in the mesh with the crowd, the mob and at that time, you have to behave yourself, according to their interest, mould yourself according to the environment, the situation and try yourself at the favourable time to forget your identity of the crowd, otherwise you won't find yourself with them and you will disappear.

46

Target

It is the meaning of your life, to live, to have it, to make you busy for the fulfillment of your dream. If you don't have a target, how are you living then? It's very difficult to pass even a minute, if you don't have any aim. It's better to die, to make your dream come true than to live without any.

We all have different reasons to live and this reason makes us fight, for the betterment of our life. You should be clear with your target to make you capable of it. A dream with no sense cannot be made sensible with your endless effort, so believe in that which is practical, have a firm stand on the ground.

Running behind the light is not possible, you cannot travel at the speed of thinking, so, superficial things are not to be given importance, they could not be important as your target or aim of life, as your dream. It will remain untouched but you will lose your valuable time. Different people have different approach and attitude to make their dream come true. Their attitude would be positive or negative but their desire is the same. Whom you will call, the man having the killer instinct?

Targets or aims are the milestones of your life and you have to go through it, to attain them. Some of them remain, till your end but this doesn't mean you had not fought for it, but it proves, it was beyond your reach with your capabilities or your dedication was incomplete.

Dream and dedication are the swiftest way to get success in reaching your target. If you believe in a dream you will set a target to it, to make it real from the virtual but this requires your dedication too, otherwise you will find yourself stranded in your dream. Making yourself clear with your goal and taking time to understand yourself that, how best is your decision to attain it, for your betterment or is it vague to fight for it, in the excitement and killing your precious time. If you find yourself with these answers, then what is left is to attack, to get it and then it makes sense for your reason to fight.

Working on half-planned target with your impractical decisions won't give you a gain, but reduce your balance of decision-making. So, why do you want to take yourself, in that direction in which you have never gone and have the feeling that you might disappear in the mesh.

"I want to have a target, till my end, so that I feel, I am breathing. Target makes me feel that I am still lagging and there are lots of things to do. It invokes in me a will to fight, you will have me and if you keep on fighting, with your zeal and dedication, I will love to share with you, to be with you. Give me the sense, to widen my horizon of thinking to set targets for me, for my betterment of life".

47

Stairs

It is the media in your house by which you change your location in the vertical direction, might be up or down, as per your need. If we don't have it, we will have only longitudinal and lateral movement and our necessity to touch the roof remains in our heart.

Everybody has this desire to have a ladder for him, for his growth, development and in search for it, he fights with his circumstances. It's not easy to get a chance of development in our life, more so, people who are associated with us in our life or not having any relation might have different liking for us in our development.

They don't feel happy to give me their hand, for their support to lessen my fight and to reduce my pain, with my effort. If they had helped me by providing their support, it would have been easy for me, to achieve my target, my goal, in less time. I would have saved my precious time of my life, in making myself complete and utilize it in the development of mankind and humanity.

We are related to each other for our development and we have to help each other because nobody is perfect in this world or rather would not seek help from others. If you will not help, then how could you expect from others so, if you have this power, to uplift him, put forward your helping hand in the shape of a ladder, for his journey towards success. You will feel yourself in the foundation of his success, so make yourself the ladder, to make him complete.

48

Opinion

It proves that you can think and you still give jobs to your brain, to utilize its power, to feel you can express yourself with your views. It is very important to feel and have a reason with every work, in terms of opinion.

It makes a sense to express it, rather to confine it in your heart and feel puzzled by it. Opinion shows the level of thinking, clarity of the subject and development of the brain.

Your views are important for me to make me complete and to know my mistakes because this could be possible, I am unable to judge my own. You have your right to express your opinion, for what you feel good or bad.

"Opinion could be embedded with positive thinking; attitude or negative thinking and it has a different impact on your life and others too. To keep a person in your life, as associated and having a quality of a critic, with his views, opinions might be beneficial for you, for your complete development, because all your weakness, would be then in front of you and if you will have a positive sense to listen to them and ask him, that do I really have limitations on me?"

Opinion is the fast track's conclusion made by a person, from his experience. So, it has an importance because if we have an opinion in hand, regarding the work, a person or anything, we can come to a conclusion, effectively.

49

Confession

You will feel happy from your heart while you opt to confess. It is not an easy task to make your mind bold, for this decision to confess, but if you believe in the soul and feel pain for others and cannot sleep while someone is in a problem, because of you, then you will not think twice to say, I'm guilty, I'm the culprit.

You will have to face trial, the punishment but you will not feel pain, because now you believe that you have to bear the consequences of your sin and you cannot see someone else to bear it, for you. "I want to reduce the pain of my sin, by confessing that I am responsible and now I am ready to face and bear, for my mistakes."

Running from your responsibility or by committing mistakes, knowingly, you won't run for long, that you also know, from your heart. So why don't you stop yourself and think that, you are wrong. I cannot run without any direction and it makes me puzzled that I am running, leaving myself behind.

I want to take myself along with me, if I don't want to betray myself and I love my soul then I will definitely come forward to say, "I am here to accept the outcome of my mistakes." You will feel changed while accepting and you will love yourself that you have that boldness to confess and now you will change everything, so, that you can face yourself and feel that you have found yourself.

50

Weapon

It is being made for your safety and for mankind. But nowadays it has become the symbol of power, to facilitate your unlawful deeds. We had invented so, to protect the mankind but it has become the killer of mankind too. We are unsafe because of this tool now, as it has come at the hands of a killer brain, for the purpose of destruction.

To keep yourself safe now, you have to learn the operation of weapons. If it is a symposium then you have to be a good orator with best views but if it is a place, where you have to talk, negotiate and deal with criminals then you should have the knowledge of weapons and its operation because they will not understand the values or ethics but they do understand the meaning of bullets and arms. You have to talk to them in their language, to save yourself and the innocent people. If he has to go from the world to save the millions then he must go. Ethics and values of life are to be discussed with them, who have the sense and the knowledge to understand it, otherwise they will kill you. Don't spoil a minute, when you have to talk in terms of bullets. Put your ethics apart and go ahead, otherwise you and your ethics would have no meaning for anyone and you will be known as past.

The bullet has no religion, caste, sense and feeling, when some intellectual brain made it, its purpose was clear in his mind, but it was redefined again, by the few, for their sake. The tool has now become the purpose of destruction and the mankind is in danger. We have to talk and think again that we are on the verge of destruction; if we on believing that the weapons are our friends. We would be no more, if we don't think now, its values and its importance in our life.

Things of destruction cannot be made the purpose of construction and you have to clear yourself, the meaning of destruction and construction. To grasp the power, you have made so, but you have forgotten the destructive weapons have the same reaction to you, as you have thought for others "One's who leave the sword, dies by the sword". So, be aware, as you are playing with fire and fire only knows how to burn. The future of the mankind is in danger and you are also not safe. Just think of it, before it becomes too late to think upon.

You have to spread love in the nature and not the radiation of chemicals, to kill someone or everyone, then how would you live alone. Use the tool for its positive aspects; otherwise you too will be destroyed with its reaction. It has a necessity in our life, for the purpose of safety and security and its important to keep it, in our life should be for a positive reason. Make yourself clear with the purpose, meaning and the result of using the weapons, before you touch them. Never touch them in your excitement, otherwise you will feel guilty of yourself, with the result.

51

Fear

Why do we fear? What is the meaning of fear? What is our state, when we feel fear? Defining fear or phobia is easier than to feel it. In the state of fear, we lose our confidence, expression and feeling but we do feel something, which is hidden that we cannot see, but we presume that thing as visible and have a presence in our life.

The things which are clear to us, we find ourselves confident, to express it, from our heart and mind but there are few or certain things which we are not able to make ourselves clear about and feel puzzled by them, in our daily life. If you will try to know the existence of that thing, its meaning, origin and its importance in your life, then you will feel that, you are developing confidence against it and now you have understood about it. Your feeling would get changed gradually and now you will not be afraid of it. We all feel fear of death because we don't want to lose this life, we want to live this life forever but we failed to do so, to avail this.

As death is the fact that has to come to all the living beings so, why don't we make ourselves clear with this bitter fact? We don't have to fear death but we have to give love to our lives, as long as we are alive.

Few of us feel fear of their life and they love to hug their death, by committing suicide or attempting it. You won't get solution for your problem, if you think like an immature mind, an undeveloped personality. You have to fight with your life, for your life, to finding a solution of your problem and not to feel fear of your problem and giving up your life, by accepting death. You will be called fools, if you compromise with your problem by giving up your precious life, that you won't get again, then why don't you love your life, by proving to fight with the problem.

Fear has no existence, if you dare to fight with it, otherwise you will be killed by your fear, one day. If it becomes sure that you are going to die then, fear of death, will make you unstable to accept your death, your acceptance of your death should be with a smile on your face that you know you are going to die and give her a strong hug, so that death feels, you don't feel fear of her and now you want to be, with her.

You can define fear as an abstract feeling but we made it existent, in our life, with our incomplete knowledge, belief and myth. Until we made ourselves aware of it, we won't feel confident about it and it will keep on living, in our heart, in our feeling as fear. We feel fear to speak truth because we don't have courage to face the world and that's the reason, we live in illusion and we die with a lie.

If because of you someone could be in problem then you have to break the silence to speak the truth, that you are responsible for it and you don't feel fear to accept it.

52

Idle

It is the state, when you don't have to do anything or you don't want to do anything. You just want to be present, not for the work, but for nothing. You don't believe in working and feel happy with having no work.

Your identity is very unclear because you have not proven yourself with the work. To prove your capabilities, you have to come out of this state otherwise you will remain same, in your state and status and will find yourself deteriorating.

If you remain idle, you won't survive for long, because to run a life, you always require an aim, a goal, to make it your target, to achieve and to make you busy too, otherwise it's very tough to pass even a minute, sitting idle for a person, who loves to work.

It is the quality of a coward and not of a brave man because cowards don't have the power to express themselves but a brave person won't sit idle, for long. He knows conquering with your work, with your effort and enthusiasm is the only fittest solution of the problem, to make you the winner of the race. If you remain idle you will find one day that all your creativity, your power to dream, your zeal to fight, you're thinking to make you bright has left you. Even your life will leave you soon, if you don't find yourself, about your idleness.

Your development, to have a have healthy life depends on you and your business with your work, but your idleness has a strong relation with your deteriorating life and your status. Only performing result oriented work can bring you out of this state of mind and you will find that you are living a healthy and prosperous life.

53

Differences

It is true, we all have different sets and levels of brain and our power to think or recognize the problem and finding the solution. We have our liking and disliking and it's our nature that every person has a different perception of things, of defining things.

You have no right to impose your opinion on someone else because he has his own liking and thinking. If you impose your thoughts on someone, you will develop complexity and differences. Differences could lead you to depart from him, so it is better to give the weight, the value to everyone, to make them feel that they and their thoughts are equally important for you.

The differences won't give you a gain in your relation or with your work but it reduces the affection, the caring and the transparency with your love. Resolving of differences shows that, you know the meaning of the relation and you don't want to spoil it, for anything.

If you are not able to judge your mistakes, within time, your differences in opinion could become the differences with someone. Opinions are your personal property and everybody who has vision to think, has his right to express his own opinion. So, this is sure, we will have different opinions on the same subject and we should feel happy that, we have views from all the brains.

We won't develop differences, if we are clear from our heart that we are discussing for the betterment of our life, for our work.

54

Addiction

Addiction is a habit. You are responsible, if you are on the wrong track because it will lead you towards your destruction slowly. It's a fact we are responsible for our mistakes because we don't think before we commit but we do think after we commit, in the shape of bad result.

Addiction makes you busy with day-to-day deterioration because you have lost your sense of thinking and capability to save yourself. Until you feel from your heart that, is it really the necessity of your life, the demand of your life, to make you live. Will you die without it or you will die, with it, you have to decide, for your betterment because you are responsible for it, as it is your interest, your liking, so you have to reply.

Until you make yourself answerable, you won't feel anything for your habit and addiction. You should feel from your heart that is it really the need of your life or your life is incomplete without it. If not, then don't waste your time to see the, outcome. Just make yourself bold and feel that, you can live without it. If it is not your need and necessity, then why are you sticking to it? And made yourself dependent on it.

One day you will find yourself very small in front of it because of your dependence and at that time, it will be tough for you to regain your strength and life. Define yourself with your need and necessity, you will find you are clear with everything, which is associated with you and you know the meaning of it and its importance in your life.

Only those people are said to be addicted, who don't want to think of their paths, which they have opted otherwise, addiction has no meaning for those, who have courage to fight, sense to think that, what's right and what's wrong. If you can distinguish between the two you won't opt for the worst and you will save yourself, your life from the problems ahead. Leave it now, before it becomes too late for you to think.

If you love yourself, you will not hesitate to at least think that are you incomplete without it. It is only a momentary enjoyment or pleasure because it does not have life, for your life, it is with you, not for you but only a filler, of your expression and it has no meaning for your life. Addiction is permanent, until you have not thought of it. So, just begin to think for your betterment of life.

55

Tears

It is the reaction of our body to relieve the pain. If we don't have this feature with us, it becomes very tough to release the pressure, the depression and the trauma of our mind.

Few drops of tears from our eyes can release the heaviness of tones from our heart. Grief, sorrow and the happiness too are the state of our mind in which we find ourselves emotionally bound and tears make a relation with our heart and our mind with the situation, environment and circumstances.

Feeling pain for someone, it shows your affection for him, care for him, but we never cry at the death of a person, whom we don't know, even after looking at his dead body. We feel pain for only those to whom we are associated to and have importance in our life.

Feeling important for someone and finding him in problem makes you depressed and you realize that how important he is, for you, in your life. This is also a fact that tears might come out of our eyes at the time of happiness, joy, this shows that how emotional we are, from our heart.

A person having has these qualities, are not hard enough on their heart, they cannot take the hard decisions about someone, with their relation because they think from their heart and not from there's brain and it's wrong. You cannot be a good decisive person, if you use your heart more than your brain. Your heart is to feel only and your brain is to act, for your betterment.

56

Death

The end point of your life after which there is complete darkness, you don't know where you are, with whom you are and how you are? We feel pain till we live, after which we don't have the sense to feel.

It's a fact that death is the cycle of life, where life ends, death takes over and we don't know the phase of this stage. We feel fear to accept the fact of death, but death never feels anything while meeting you and taking you along with her.

You have to believe this, who has taken birth has to go one day and your fear to accept this fact, will make you die before your death. If you believe in this fact, you will accept your death happily and that makes you more competent to understand the meaning of it.

Life is temporary but death is permanent. You do, or try to do, every style of malpractices with your work, for you and for the betterment of your life, irrespective of thinking that for which you are thinking most, by every means, has a very temporary standing, that is your life.

You don't know about your tomorrow, what could happen to you, in your life, it's totally unclear to everyone about his tomorrow. Life is definitely going to ditch you, either today or tomorrow but death will never ditch you, because it does not have a reversible phase from death to life again. Once dead you have to be in death mode always and even if you try or think to come out of it, you cannot. If this is a fact and it is being clear to you then try to live your life, in total.

A meaningful life has a fragrance of love, faith and trust and you will never think of wasting, even a minute of your precious life. It is better to discuss and think more of life because we don't have much to discuss about death. In life, we have sense, feeling of pain, love and everything, if we think, we are living otherwise you can feel that without these your life has no meaning.

Before death, I want to think only about my life so that; my life gives me lots of love and care, to make me feel that I have lived a full and meaningful life till my end. It takes years to make a person stand on his feet's but a killer mind makes him dead, in a minute, this is called the premature death and the person having no sense or pain while killing others is considered to be living with a retarded mind, a dead without emotions.

You can do anything or everything, when you are living, you can change yourself for the sake of others, you can try to make them change, for yourself, so try with your every effort, in your living mode otherwise you will feel regret at the time of death. You can have a desire that you want to live every minute of your life, till your end and feel alive at the time of death.

Testimonials

"No aspect of life is out of reach of this book. Each topic defines life, teaches life and creates a new you. The work is comparable to the best in the world, if we talk about this genre of writing. It's not just another self help book that is incomprehensible but while reading you will find it to be a page out of your life. Each chapter of this book takes you a step closer to yourself. This book is a journey, and at the final stop the reader finds himself......smiling".

Dr. Kumar Vishwas
Poet & Aam Aadmi Party – Leader

"Bitter Truth".

Ar. Nidhi Wadhwa
Director: Wadhwa Associates, Agra

"This book is a cook book. It has all the ingredients we need to lead a successful life and gives us the recipe for using them in appropriate proportions".

Ms. Vidhi Sobti
Student, New Delhi

"The author seems to have experience the life watchfully and have observed the interpersonal aspect of life very carefully. It seems to be a nice piece of work and practicing these components of life one can live happily".

Dr. Nachiketa Mishra
Head HR, IME Group of Education, New Delhi

"The book leads to introspection and enlightens every reader. The author has covered every aspect of life in a very structured manner, which is easily understood. The book is a piece of art and promise for a better environment filled with love, joy and happiness. It promises a world where people will feel valued and encouraged".

Mr. Rohit Sehgal
Tata Motors, New Delhi

"The author has skillfully touched the chapters of his book and if values being inculcated in our daily lives will improve our relationships and lead to a better society".

Ms. Priya Sehgal
Teacher of Mater Dei School, New Delhi

"Life is precious." The author has beautified the definition of life with his efforts. It is indeed an excellent piecework. I give my sincere thanks to the author, who has given us a gem in shape of this book".

Mr. Karmvir Singh
Yamaha Motors, New Delhi

"After reading the first page of the book........I thought to go to home and complete it before sleep. Love you Pravin! Sweet Gift".

Mr. Mir Nasir Ali Khan
Managing Director, MAK Projects, Hyderabad.
www.makprojects.com

"How could the life be defined in few pages I have understood it after going through this book".

Ms. Aakanksha Rajpoot
Student, Amity International School, Gurgaon

"Book starts from the chapter "LIFE" and ends at "DEATH", I have travelled through the pages one by one and smiled at last...........genre is indeed appreciable. People who are running from the LIFE can at least spare some time to this before taking any decision".

Dr. Sanjeev Gemawat
New Delhi